SADLIER'S
Coming to Faith Program

COMING TO
GOD'S LOVE

Dr. Gerard F. Baumbach

Dr. Eleanor Ann Brownell

Moya Gullage

Joan B. Collins

Helen Hemmer, I. H. M.

Gloria Hutchinson

Dr. Norman F. Josaitis

Rev. Michael J. Lanning, O. F. M.

Dr. Marie Murphy

Karen Ryan

Joseph F. Sweeney

The Ad Hoc Committee
to Oversee the Use of the Catechism,
National Conference of Catholic Bishops,
has found this catechetical text to be
in conformity with the
Catechism of the Catholic Church.

with

Dr. Thomas H. Groome
Boston College

Official Theological Consultant
The Most Rev. Edward K. Braxton, Ph. D., S. T. D.

Scriptural Consultant
Rev. Donald Senior, C. P., Ph. D., S. T. D.

Catechetical and Liturgical Consultants
Dr. Gerard F. Baumbach
Dr. Eleanor Ann Brownell

Pastoral Consultants
Rev. Msgr. John F. Barry
Rev. Virgilio P. Elizondo, Ph. D., S. T. D.

Catechetical Assessment Consultant
Dr. George Elford

William H. Sadlier, Inc.
9 Pine Street
New York, New York 10005–1002

Nihil Obstat
✠ Most Reverend George O. Wirz
Censor Librorum

Imprimatur
✠ Most Reverend William H. Bullock
Bishop of Madison
May 9, 1997

The *Nihil Obstat* and *Imprimatur* are official declarations that a book or pamphlet is free of doctrinal or moral error. No implication is contained therein that those who have granted the *Nihil Obstat* and *Imprimatur* agree with the contents, opinions, or statements expressed.

Printed in the United States of America.

Credits appear on page 304.

Home Office:
9 Pine Street
New York, NY 10005–1002

ISBN: 0-8215-4304-0
23456789/98

DEAR YOUNG PEOPLE,

Your new religion book is called **Coming to God's Love.** It is written to help you grow in living as a friend of Jesus Christ and a member of his Church.

Coming to God's Love tells how the commandments of God and the teachings of Jesus Christ help us to live happily and freely as God's people.

It teaches us that we share the responsibility for building the kingdom, or reign, of God in our world today.

When you use this book, ask the Holy Spirit to help you to

- be a faithful follower of Jesus Christ;
- live faithfully the commandments of God and of the Church;
- find ways that you can be a sign of God's love to everyone;
- thank God by your words and actions for the gift of his love;
- think about ways Jesus wants you to continue his work and be a peacemaker.

We hope that you will enjoy learning how God wants us to live. We pray that you will continue to grow in God's love always.

All of Us in the Sadlier Family

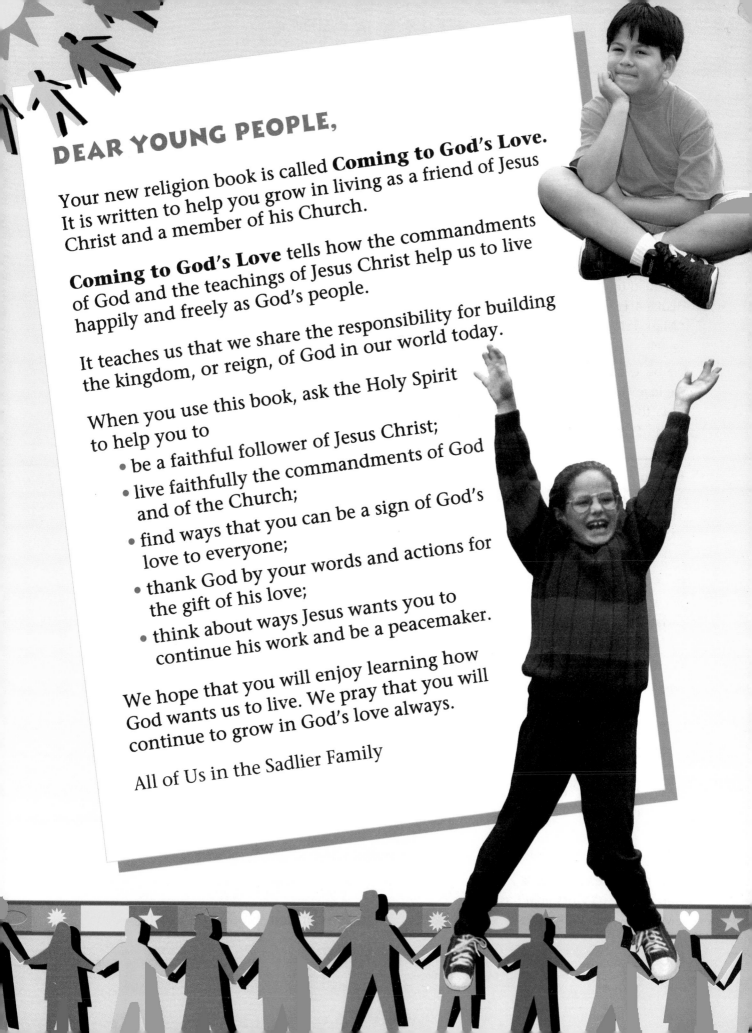

CONTENTS

Unit 1   Living as a Catholic Christian   page

Doctrine: Catholic Teaching

Unit 1 Review and Unit 1 Test—see pages 262–263

| Unit 4 | We Live as Christians | page |

Doctrine: Catholic Teaching

OPENING PRAYER SERVICE

A Prayer of Praise

Leader: Welcome to a new year together as we begin to explore even more about our faith as Catholics.

Take a moment and look at the cover of your new religion book. What do the shells remind you of? For many people, a shell is a reminder of the water used in the sacrament of Baptism and the promises that we have made to live as disciples of Jesus.

How does Jesus want us to live as his disciples? Let us listen to his words:

Reader 1: "If anyone wishes to come after me, he must deny himself and take his cross daily and follow me" (Luke 9:23).

Leader: What a challenge Jesus gives us! We will have to be strong if we are to be disciples of Jesus. Let us bless ourselves with the holy water contained in this shell and renew the promises we made at Baptism.

(Direction: Teacher goes to each student and offers shell with holy water. Each student dips his or her finger in the water and makes the sign of the cross silently.)

Reader 2: Please respond by praying, *Lord, hear our prayer.*

God our Father, help us to be free from sin and live as your children.

All: Lord, hear our prayer.

Reader 3: Jesus, Son of God, help us to carry our cross with love, as you did.

All: Lord, hear our prayer.

Reader 4: God the Holy Spirit, grant us wisdom and understanding so that we may grow as strong disciples of Jesus and faithful members of his Church.

All: Lord, hear our prayer.

Leader: We cannot grow as strong disciples of Jesus by ourselves. We need the community of the Church. Together let us pray as members of the Church in the words our Savior gave us.

All: (Pray the Lord's Prayer.)

Called by Name

OUR LIFE

Think for a minute. What does it mean for you to have a name?

Your parents probably thought and talked about many names before they chose the one that was to be yours. Why is a name so important? Wouldn't a number do just as well?

How do you feel about your name?

HELLO MY NAME IS:

HELLO MY NAME IS: ELISA

HELLO MY NAME IS: Paul

SHARING LIFE

Each one of us here has a name that is ours alone. How many people in our group can you name?

Stand in a circle. Take turns walking around the inside of the circle. When the music stops, or when your teacher says to stop, the "walker" must find out and name the person in front of him or her. Everyone else in the circle should repeat the name correctly and with respect.

In the Gospel of Luke we read the wonderful story about the angel Gabriel coming from God to ask Mary to be the mother of the Savior. The angel said to Mary, "Hail favored one! The Lord is with you. Behold you will conceive in your womb and bear a son, and you will name him Jesus."
Luke 1:28,31

The name Jesus means "God saves." Jesus came to save and to give new life to all people. Whenever we say the name of Jesus, we remember that he is our Savior. This is the reason we show great respect for the holy name of Jesus. We never use this name except in saying our prayers or in sharing our faith.

Each of us has an individual name that identifies who we are. These are the very names by which God calls us. In the Bible we read, "I have called you by name: you are Mine" (Isaiah 43:1).

We also share a common name that identifies us as disciples of Jesus Christ. We are called Christians; we follow Jesus Christ. We carry his name to identify who we are.

This year we will learn much more about what it means to follow Jesus Christ in the Church. We will grow together in following his way and in living for the kingdom of God.

At the World Youth Day in Denver, Colorado, Pope John Paul II spoke to young people from all over the world about what it means to be a follower of Jesus Christ. He said:

"Young people from every corner of the world, you have opened your hearts to the truth of Christ's promise of new life. You, young pilgrims, have also shown that you understand that Christ's gift of life is not for you alone. . . . Place your intelligence, your talents, your enthusiasm, your compassion, and your strength at the service of life!"

From "A Celebration of Life,"
Pope John Paul II

To follow Jesus means:

- to cherish and care for the gift of your own life;

- to defend and support the lives of other people;

- to live your life following the example of Jesus.

This year we will be "pilgrims"— people on a journey with Jesus Christ. We will explore ways that we can use our intelligence, our enthusiasm, our concern for others, and our strengths to live and share the life that Jesus our Savior came to give to all people.

Coming To Faith

You are a Christian. Talk together about what the name Christian means to you. Create a personal symbol or word that shows what it means to you to be a disciple of Jesus Christ.

Practicing Faith

Come together in a prayer circle and take turns sharing your symbols. Then pray together:

† Jesus, you have called us by name. We are yours. We want to be your disciples and to share your life with our world.

Now make a garland of your symbols by pasting them, one by one, on a long piece of yarn or string.

Keep your garland in a place where you will see it next time you meet.

Talk with your teacher about ways you and your family can share the "Faith Alive" section. Talk to your family about your personal Christian symbol. Make a family Christian symbol.

REVIEW

Christian Symbols

Talk with your family about what being a Christian means to you. Explain the symbol you made. Together make a family symbol. Design it in the space below.

FAITH ALIVE AT HOME AND IN THE PARISH

This year your son or daughter will explore in depth what it means to live as a disciple of Jesus. He or she will learn what it means to follow him by living as a member of the Catholic Church. Within the Church community we support one another in following the way of Jesus by living according to the Ten Commandments, the Law of Love, the Beatitudes, and the Works of Mercy. You will want to continue to take an active role in guiding your child's growth in Christian faith.

Learn by heart **Faith Summary**

- We are called Christians because we are disciples of Jesus Christ.

- We are called to share Jesus' life with others.

- We show respect for the holy name of Jesus.

1 Living for God's Kingdom

Jesus, help us to make God's kingdom come on earth.

Our Life

Every day we hear bad news and good news about our world. What bad news have you heard recently? What good news?

Pretend you are a TV reporter. The TV camera is focused on these two pictures. Give a report of what is happening in each scene.

Sharing Life

Talk together about ways the bad things in our world might be changed to good things.

Do you think they can be changed? Why or why not?

Imagine Jesus is sitting in our group right now. What do you think he might say to us about the good and bad things in our world?

Making Our World Better

Now imagine that Jesus asks you to do something to help make the world a better place.

Think for a moment. Then write your idea on a slip of paper. Put your paper in a box with those of your friends. Take turns picking a slip from the box. Read each one aloud.

Talk together about ways you think fourth graders can respond to Jesus' request.

This week we will learn more about what it means to build God's kingdom.

We Will Learn

- Jesus Christ preached the good news of God's kingdom.

- The kingdom is the saving power of God's life and love in the world.

- Catholics are called to build up God's kingdom.

Jesus, help us to be builders of God's kingdom on earth.

Do you think our world is the way God wants it to be? Why or why not?

The Kingdom of God

When Jesus was about thirty years old, he left his home to begin his mission, or task, of preaching his good news to the world.

The good news Jesus preached was that God loves all people and that the kingdom of God had come in him.

One Sabbath day Jesus went to the synagogue in Nazareth. When invited to read, he found and then read this passage from the Scriptures:

"The Spirit of the Lord is upon me,
 because he has anointed me
  to bring glad tidings to the poor.
He has sent me to proclaim
  liberty to captives
 and recovery of sight to the blind,
to let the oppressed go free,
  and to proclaim a year acceptable
  to the Lord."

When Jesus finished reading, he rolled up the scroll and sat down. Everyone in the synagogue was looking at him. The excitement grew. Then Jesus said, "Today this scripture passage is fulfilled in your hearing."

Everyone was amazed. Jesus was saying that this great Scripture reading had come true in him. The people began to whisper to one another, "Isn't this the son of Joseph?" They did not believe that Jesus was the Son of God, sent by God the Father to bring about the kingdom of justice and peace.
Based on Luke 4:16–22

The kingdom, or reign, of God is the saving power of God's life and love in the world. It is the good news that he loves us and is always with us. God does not want any people to be hungry, hurting, or treated unfairly.

We must do what we can to bring about the kind of world that God wants. We do God's loving will to show others that his kingdom has come!

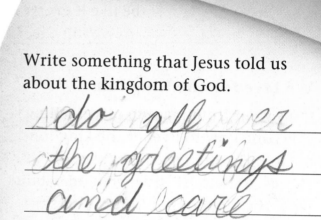

Write something that Jesus told us about the kingdom of God.

do all over the greetings and care to the poor

Scrolls

In the time of Jesus, people wrote on pieces of leather, parchment, or paper made from the papyrus plant. A scroll was made from sheets of these materials sewn together.

How would you describe the kingdom of God?

What will you do today to show your family and neighborhood that the kingdom of God is here?

OUR CATHOLIC FAITH

▪ Holy Spirit, strengthen us to proclaim the good news of Jesus.

▪ What would our world be like if everyone tried to live in peace?

We Live for the Kingdom

Jesus went from place to place, telling everyone how to live for the kingdom of God. He often used parables, or stories, to help His listeners understand what the kingdom of God was like.

Here are two parables that Jesus told about the kingdom, or reign, of God.

One parable says that the kingdom of God is like a treasure hidden in a field. When someone finds this treasure, that person sells everything to buy the field. Then the person owns the most valuable treasure of all.

Another parable says that the kingdom of God is like a pearl of great price. When someone finds an unusually beautiful pearl, that person will sell everything in order to buy the pearl.

Based on Matthew 13:44–46

These parables help us to understand that doing God's loving will must come first in our lives.

We must be part of God's kingdom of love and justice here on earth, so that we can be forever with God in the kingdom of heaven.

When Jesus talked about the kingdom of God, some did not understand what He really meant. They thought that He was talking about a country or a kingdom where Jesus would be an earthly king.

Even some of Jesus' disciples were slow to understand. One day, two of them came to Jesus. They said, "When you sit on Your throne in Your glorious kingdom, we want You to let us sit with You, one at Your right and one at Your left."

Mark 10:37

The **kingdom**, or **reign**, **of God** is the saving power of his life and love in the world.

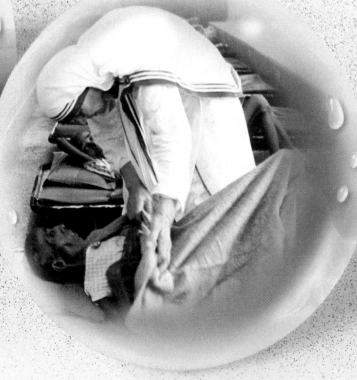

These disciples did not see the real meaning of the kingdom. Jesus tells us that the kingdom of God is not a place. It is living so that all who see us know what it means to do God's loving will. God's will is what is best for us and what he wants for us here and now.

God wants us to make Jesus the most important part of our lives. We are to serve others as Jesus did. We are to be his disciples and follow his way. Jesus has called everyone to come together around him and in his name. We cannot work for God's kingdom or do his will without Jesus. In Jesus, the kingdom of God is made present.

As Jesus' disciples, we do God's will when we take responsibility for loving others and caring for our world. Doing God's will now is the way we help to bring about the kingdom of God that Jesus announced. We live as Jesus' disciples and hope to share in the kingdom of heaven forever.

What is the greatest treasure in your life? What would Jesus say about your choice?

Choose some ways that fourth graders can work for the kingdom of God today.

OUR CATHOLIC FAITH

- Loving God, help us to show your saving love to others.

- Why are you so important to God's kingdom?

We Can Make a Difference

Jesus told everyone, "This is the time of fulfillment. The kingdom of God is at hand. Repent, and believe in the gospel" (Mark 1:15).

When some people heard Jesus speak like this about the kingdom of God, they tried to change their lives. Many left everything and followed Jesus.

Other people who heard Jesus decided to give up their bad ways. They turned away from sin and began to do God's will. They began to know the saving power of God's life and love in the world. They began to see the importance of God's kingdom. But others found the message of Jesus too hard to accept and walked away.

The words of Jesus are meant for us, too. As faithful members of the Church and guided by the pope and bishops, we, too, can turn away from sin. We can make a decision to care about the kingdom of God.

Even the smallest thing we do for the kingdom of God will make a difference in ourselves and in our world.

We can build up God's kingdom by:

- believing the good news.

- following Jesus.

- avoiding sin.

- loving others and ourselves.

- working for justice and peace in our world.

Thy Kingdom Come

When Jesus founded the Church, he told Saint Peter, "I will give you the keys to the kingdom of heaven" (Matthew 16:19). Under the leadership of Peter and his successors, the Church would continue to proclaim the good news of God's kingdom in every age until the end of the world.

At the end of the world, Jesus will come again. Then the last judgement will take place. Jesus will judge us according to the way we have lived our lives as his followers.

Those who have died in God's grace and friendship will be rewarded with heaven. Those who have freely chosen to reject God will be separated from him for all eternity. This separation is called hell.

Those who are not yet ready for heaven but who died in God's grace and friendship must experience a period of purification to prepare them for heaven. This is called purgatory. God does not wish anyone to be separated from him. We ask God to help us choose a life that will lead us to heaven.

Learn by heart Faith Summary

- Jesus preached the good news of the kingdom of God.

- The kingdom of God is the saving power of God's life and love in the world.

- We build up the kingdom of God by working for love, justice, and peace in our world.

COMING TO FAITH

We are followers of Jesus Christ. We are called to help build up the kingdom of God.

What can fourth graders do to:

- share the good news of Jesus?

- work for justice?

- be peacemakers?

PRACTICING FAITH

Go on a treasure hunt to find the real meaning of the kingdom of God. Draw a dotted line to show the route your ship will take. Avoid the things that will keep you from the kingdom. Stop at the things that will help you reach your goal. After the treasure hunt, gather together and pray the Our Father.

Treasure of the Kingdom of God

caring for God's gifts

making peace

fighting

making fun of someone

helping at home

disobeying rules

Start

Talk with your teacher about ways you and your family might use the "Faith Alive" section. Then pray the Our Father together.

REVIEW ■ TEST

Circle the letter beside the correct answer.

1. Jesus often explained the kingdom by telling

   a. poems.

   b. parables.

   c. biographies.

2. The power of God's life and love in the world is the

   a. kingdom of God.

   b. Old Testament.

   c. Church.

3. One parable Jesus told said the kingdom of God is like a

   a. pearl of great price.

   b. synagogue.

   c. throne.

4. Another parable compared the kingdom to a

   a. parent.

   b. fisherman.

   c. treasure hidden in a field.

5. How can we build up God's kingdom?

_____

_____

2 | The Virtues of Faith, Hope, and Love

Loving God, help us to trust in you.

OUR LIFE

"Loving God, teach me to trust in You." This was the prayer of a great saint, Teresa of Avila. It is a prayer that we, too, can pray often.

Teresa lived in Spain in the 16th century. She was beautiful, friendly, bright—and funny, too. She blended great reverence with down-to-earth honesty in her conversations with God. She often let God know when God seemed to be asking a lot of her. Yet she drew strength from God's presence in her life and in the world around her. Everything in nature spoke to Teresa of God's presence and love. In one of her prayers she wrote:

"O God, how you show forth your power in giving courage to a little ant!"

What do you think Teresa saw an ant doing that caused her to praise God?

Do you ever find signs that God is present in the world? What are they?

SHARING LIFE

What do you think is the best way to show trust in God?

What are some things that make it hard to trust in God?

24

Teresa of Avila's life wasn't always easy. Often she had to make long journeys traveling in all sorts of weather, against many difficulties and dangers. Through it all she kept her sense of humor and her trust in God. Here is some advice she gave us.

Let nothing disturb you.
Let nothing frighten you.
All things are passing
    but God never changes.
Patience gains all things.
If you have God, you
    need nothing else.

Talk together about Saint Teresa's advice. What does it tell you about trust in God?

This week we will learn more about the virtues of faith, hope, and love.

We Will Learn

- We have faith and hope in God.

- We love God, ourselves, and our neighbors as ourselves.

- Faith, hope, and love are virtues that help us live as true Christians.

Our Catholic Faith

Dear God, make our faith strong.

Share with a friend why faith in God is important to you.

Faith in God

We can always trust a loving parent. Even more so, we can always believe and trust in God. God will always love us and care for us.

Jesus explained why we can have such faith in God. Jesus said, "Look at the birds in the sky; they do not sow or reap. . . yet your heavenly Father feeds them. Are not you more important than they?"(Matthew 6:26).

Jesus then showed how God cares for us as a loving parent cares for a child. Jesus told them that their Father in heaven knows all that they need and that God would care for them.
Based on Matthew 6:32–33

When we have faith in God, we believe and trust in God, who loves and cares for us. Having faith helps us to make good choices so that we live as disciples of Jesus Christ.

Hope in God

We must also have hope in God. Hope helps us never to give up, no matter what happens to us, our family, or our world. Our faith gives us this confidence, or strong trust, in God's love.

Christians also have hope that God will give us eternal life. *Eternal life* means living forever with God in heaven.

Jesus said to them, "Whoever hears my word and believes in the one who sent me has eternal life" (John 5:24).

Our world needs us to share Jesus' message of faith and hope. We must do what we can to overcome sin and evil.

FAITH WORD

A **virtue** is the habit of doing good.

People who are hungry, poor, or treated unjustly need to see that we are trying to help them.

We must also show others that if we have faith and hope in God, we can bring about God's kingdom now and live forever with God in heaven.

Explain what it means for you to have faith and hope in God.

How will your faith and hope in God help you make good choices today?

27

Our Catholic Faith

- Loving God, we believe and trust in you.

- Tell some ways that you show love each day for God, yourself, and others.

"You shall love the Lord, your God, with all your heart, with all your being, with all your strength, and with all your mind, and your neighbor as yourself" (Luke 10:27).

This teaching is called the Law of Love. We sometimes call it the Great Commandment. This kind of love means that we live in peace and justice with our family, our classmates, and everyone else.

Love of God

Each day we need to make good choices to follow the way that Jesus showed us. We need faith and hope in God to do this. But even more, we need love.

The night before Jesus died, he was telling his disciples how they could carry on his mission of working for the kingdom, or reign, of God. He said, "Love one another. As I have loved you, so you also should love one another. This is how all will know that you are my disciples, if you have love for one another" (John 13:34–35).

The Law of Love

Jesus always taught people how to love God, one another, and themselves. He said that the commandment to love was the greatest teaching of the Scriptures.

The Law of Love means that we treat every person as our neighbor. It also means that we share this message of love with others by the example of our own lives. Christians must try to show this love especially to people who are hungry, poor, or treated unjustly.

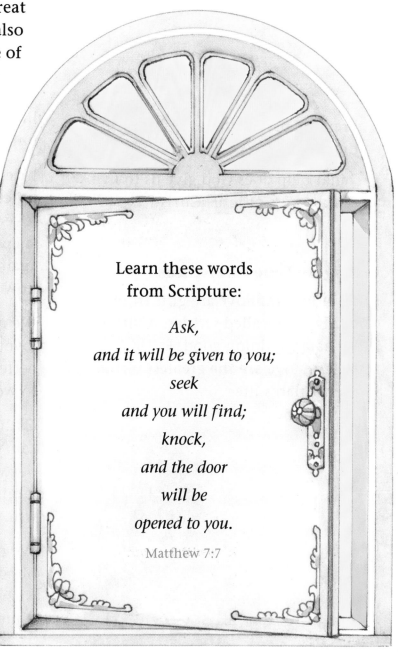

Learn these words from Scripture:

Ask,
and it will be given to you;
seek
and you will find;
knock,
and the door
will be
opened to you.

Matthew 7:7

What does the Great Commandment mean to you now?

What will you do today to show that you truly love God, yourself, and others?

OUR CATHOLIC FAITH

Pray the prayer to the Holy Spirit on page 291.

What help does God give us to live as followers of Jesus Christ?

Theo = God

Living as True Christians

Faith, hope, and love are gifts from God. They are called virtues. A virtue is the habit of doing good. Faith, hope, and love are the greatest virtues in a Christian's life.

In fact, we call these three virtues by a special name. They are the *theological virtues*. They help us to live in union with the Blessed Trinity: God the Father, God the Son, and God the Holy Spirit. The purpose of the theological virtues is that we might live God's own life of grace. Faith, hope, and love aim our lives directly toward God.

Like all habits, we do not learn to practice the virtues of faith, hope, and love overnight. But Jesus expects us to keep on trying to live them. Beginning again is more important than counting how many times we fail.

We must not use our faith, hope, and love of God to make only ourselves better. We must use these gifts of God to work together for his kingdom.

Catholics are called to work together to try to stop violence and injustice in our world, our neighborhood, or our family. We must learn to forgive those who have hurt us.

We need to learn to give up something of our own so that others may live with peace and dignity. This is what it means to live as true Christians.

The Cardinal Virtues

We know that the theological virtues are gifts from God. There are other virtues, however, that we can develop in ourselves with the help of God's grace. These are called *human virtues*. These virtues are habits that grow each and every time we try to do what is good.

In Catholic teaching, four of these virtues are very important, and for this reason they are called the *cardinal virtues*. They are prudence, justice, fortitude, and temperance.

The virtue of *prudence* gives us correct knowledge about the things we should do and the things that we should avoid. Prudence leads us to take the good advice of others.

The virtue of *justice* helps us to give all people what is due to them. A just person treats everyone fairly and respects the rights of everyone as God wants.

The virtue of *fortitude* helps us to conquer our fears and to be strong in living our faith. Fortitude also helps us to overcome difficulties in our lives.

The virtue of *temperance* helps to have discipline in our lives—in what we eat, in what we drink, and in what we do. It is important to eat, for example, but too much food or too little food can make us sick. A disciple of Jesus can enjoy the good things of life, but with the gentle control of temperance.

PRUDENCE

Pray every day that the Holy Spirit will guide you in living the four cardinal virtues.

Learn by heart Faith Summary

- Faith enables us to believe and trust in God.

- Hope enables us to have full confidence in God, no matter what happens.

- Love enables us to love God, ourselves, and our neighbors.

COMING TO FAITH

Imagine you are standing among God's gifts of nature. Sit in a relaxed position and feel God's presence and love. Finish the prayer.

† Jesus, help my faith to be as strong as. . . .

Jesus, help my hope in God to be as tall as. . . .

Jesus, help my love for God to flow as deep as. . . .

PRACTICING FAITH

Sit in a circle with your group. One at a time hold a small smooth rock in the palm of your hand. Rub it gently. To help you feel at peace, turn the rock over and over slowly in the palm of your hands. Choose one of the statements below and complete it. Then pass the rock to your neighbor. Listen carefully as each of your friends completes a chosen statement.

My faith gives me strength to. . . .

My greatest hope for myself is. . . .

For me, love is most difficult when. . . .

Talk with your teacher about ways you and your family might use the "Faith Alive" section. You might do the activity on the virtues together.

REVIEW ▪ TEST

Circle the letter beside the correct answer.

1. Virtues are

   a. sacraments.

   b. habits. *(circled)*

   c. sacramentals. *(circled)*

2. Faith, hope, and love are

   a. books of the Bible.

   b. laws.

   c. virtues. *(circled)*

3. Living forever with God is called

   a. eternal life. *(circled)*

   b. the Law of Love.

   c. hope.

4. The virtue of faith helps us to

   a. believe and trust in God. *(circled)*

   b. make easy choices.

   c. be popular.

5. Tell some ways you will live one of the cardinal virtues.

By becoming helpful

FAITH ALIVE ▪ AT HOME AND IN THE PARISH

In this chapter your fourth grader has learned about the great Christian virtues of faith, hope, and love—the theological virtues. We call these three virtues "theological" because they are gifts of God, lead us to God, and draw us into a deeper relationship with the Blessed Trinity.

Your child needs to see God's love in you and to experience these great virtues being practiced in your home. Talk as a family about ways each of you will practice these virtues better this week. Ask yourself how you can be a more loving parent to your child.

Faith, Hope, Love

Take a few minutes as a family to do this activity. Ask each one to finish these statements:

My faith in God helps me to . . .
My hope in God helps me when . . .
My love for God calls me to . . .

Then pray together:

† Glory to the Father, and to the Son,
and to the Holy Spirit.
As it was in the beginning,
is now, and will be for ever. Amen.

3 ⳨ The Church, Jesus' Community

Dear Jesus,
teach us how
to follow you.

Our Life

Simon (later called Peter), his brother Andrew, and their partners James and John had been fishing all night in the Sea of Galilee. They caught nothing.

Then Jesus came along and told them to try again. They did, and soon the boats were so filled with fish that they were almost sinking. Jesus said, "Do not be afraid; from now on you will be catching men."

Simon, Andrew, James, and John quickly pulled the boats up on the beach. Then they left everything and followed Jesus, becoming his disciples.
Based on Luke 5:1–11

Why did Simon and his friends follow Jesus?

What is it about Jesus that makes you want to follow him?

Sharing Life

Imagine you are with Simon Peter on the day that Jesus said, "Come, follow me." What might Jesus be asking you to do?

Can you follow Jesus today? How?

How do you feel as you hear Jesus say "Come, follow me?" What do you talk about with Simon, Andrew, James, and John as you start up the beach with Jesus? Are you nervous? excited? curious? Work with a partner to make up a poem, a song, or a skit to express your feelings.

Share your work with the whole group. It will help you as we learn more this week about the ways we follow Jesus as members of the Catholic Church.

✳ We Will Learn

- Jesus sent the Holy Spirit to help us.

- The Church carries on the work of Jesus.

- We belong to the Catholic Church.

Jesus, you call us as you called Peter and Andrew. We will try to follow you.

Tell something you do because you are a disciple of Jesus.

The Promise of the Spirit

Simon Peter and the other fishermen were the first disciples of Jesus. Later he called many other women and men and taught them how to live for the kingdom of God. Jesus' community of disciples was to carry on his mission of bringing the good news of God's kingdom to the world. They were also to follow his teachings and make Jesus the center of their lives.

On the night before he died, Jesus shared his last meal with his friends. He knew that he was about to die. Jesus said to them, "My children, I will be with you only a little while longer" (John 13:33).

Jesus knew that Peter and his other followers would need help to live as his disciples. They were very worried and upset and did not want Jesus to go away. Jesus told them that he would send them a Helper.

Pentecost, by Gotthard Bauer, 1988

"The Advocate, the holy Spirit that the Father will send in my name — he will teach you everything and remind you of all that [I] have told you" (John 14:26).

On the following day, Good Friday, Jesus was put to death on a cross. Many of his friends were so afraid that they ran away to hide.

A Christian **witness** is one who by faith and example shares faith in Jesus Christ with others.

The Holy Spirit Comes

After forty days, Jesus returned to his Father in heaven. Jesus' friends were together with Mary, his mother. All at once they heard a noise like a loud wind blowing. They saw what looked like tongues of fire spread out and touch each person. They were all filled with God the Holy Spirit, as Jesus promised.

Now the disciples of Jesus went forth as his witnesses. With courage, they told everyone the good news about Jesus. Many people were baptized. This is how our Church began to grow. We call this day the feast of Pentecost.

The Holy Spirit is with each of us today. When we are baptized, we receive the Holy Spirit and begin our lives as members of Jesus' community, the Church. The Holy Spirit helps us to believe and live Jesus' good news.

Three days later their fear turned into joy. Jesus was alive. Jesus had risen from the dead!

For forty days after his resurrection, Jesus appeared to his friends many times. He reminded them that soon he would go away.

- Can you act out the story of Pentecost?

- Do you know someone who needs to hear the good news of Jesus today? What good news will you share with that person?

OUR CATHOLIC FAITH

■ Come, Holy Spirit, fill us with the fire of your love.

■ When do you most need the help of the Holy Spirit?

The Church Today

Today the Church is guided by God the Holy Spirit. The Church still carries on the work of Jesus, as the first Christians did. The Church preaches and lives the good news of God's kingdom. It tells people all over the world that God loves us and is near to us.

The early Christians came together frequently to praise and worship God. They celebrated the Eucharist, the special meal that Jesus himself had given to them at the Last Supper. They celebrated Baptism to welcome new members into the Church, the body of Christ.

Today the Church is also a community of worship. We gather together to praise and thank God, our source of life and love. All over the world, our Church celebrates Mass and the sacraments. The Church also teaches us how to pray and worship God at other times.

Jesus showed his disciples how to love and serve others. The Holy Spirit helped Jesus' disciples to live the way that Jesus had shown them. They looked out for one another and shared whatever they had with those in need.

Today the Church continues Jesus' work of serving and caring for others. We remember that Jesus taught his disciples to love God with all their minds, and hearts, and strength, and to love others as they love themselves. This means that we try to love and care for others as Jesus loves and cares for us.

No one must be left out of our love. We must work for justice and peace everywhere and for everyone. We can do this only when we are strengthened and nourished by God's own life of grace. That is why it is so important for Catholics to celebrate the sacraments. By the power of the Holy Spirit, they bring us God's grace.

Today our Church reaches out to everyone and welcomes all people into Jesus' community. We try to live as a community of faith, hope, and love. We are a community nourished by the Eucharist.

The Church preaches the good news, worships God, serves others, and lives as a community of faith, hope, and love. We should be proud to belong to the Church as it tries to live the way of Jesus.

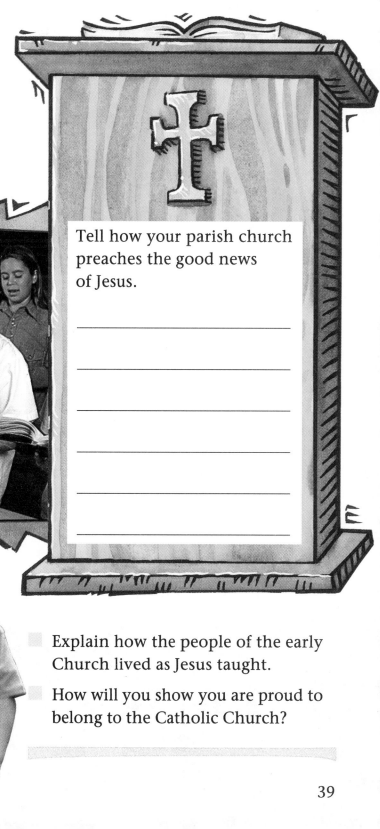

Tell how your parish church preaches the good news of Jesus.

_____

_____

_____

_____

_____

_____

Explain how the people of the early Church lived as Jesus taught.

How will you show you are proud to belong to the Catholic Church?

39

- In silence, thank Jesus for his presence among us.

- Name one thing you think Jesus is asking you to do as a member of his Church.

We Belong to the Church

Jesus said, "Where two or three are gathered together in my name, there am I in the midst of them" (Matthew 18:20). When the community of the Church gathers together, Jesus is truly with us.

We become members of the Church through Baptism. By this sacrament we are freed from the power of sin, become children of God, and are welcomed into the Church, the body of Christ. We live out our Baptism in our family, in our parish community, and in our world.

As a family, we are to love and care for one another, as Jesus teaches us.

Our parish is a community made up of all the families and other people in our neighborhood who belong to the Catholic Church. Together we worship God and live for God's kingdom.

Our parish loves and cares for all its members and for those who do not belong to the Church. We share the good news of Jesus and work for justice and peace.

All the Catholic parishes in one area make up a diocese, which is led by the bishop. All the dioceses together make up the Catholic Church, which is found throughout the whole world.

Jesus wants you to grow in living the Catholic faith all your life. Then you, too, will be able to take part in the Church's mission of preaching, worshiping, and serving.

The Great Amen

When Catholics come together as a
worshiping assembly, we gather in
the name of the Blessed Trinity.
Our prayers, especially the Mass, are
directed to the Father, through the Son,
and by the power of the Holy Spirit.

At the end of every Eucharistic Prayer,
we hear the priest pray these words
of praise and glory. As he lifts up the
Host and chalice, he says of Jesus:

> Through him,
> with him,
> in him,
> in the unity of the Holy Spirit,
> all glory and honor is yours,
> almighty Father,
> for ever and ever.

We respond together with the
Great Amen.

Before Mass this week, look through
a missalette. Find the many other
prayers that we offer to God the Father,
through the Son, by the power of
the Holy Spirit.

Learn by heart **Faith Summary**

- The Church is guided by
  the Holy Spirit.

- The Church preaches, serves,
  worships, and lives as Jesus'
  community of faith, hope,
  and love.

- We become members of the
  Church through Baptism.

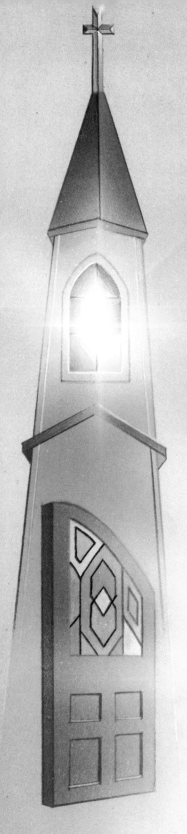

Coming To Faith

Tell how the Holy Spirit helps us in our Church to be witnesses for Jesus. Share how we spread the good news, worship, and serve others.

Then share with one another how belonging to the Church makes a difference in your life.

Practicing Faith

Work with a partner. Choose one of these words that tells what the Church does: **WITNESS; WORSHIP; SERVE.** See whether you can create an acrostic that tells what it means to you. Here is an example:

We spread the good news.

I am a member of the Church.

The Church continues Jesus' work.

Newness of life comes from the Holy Spirit.

Everyone is welcome in our Church.

Spirit-filled, the Church is found throughout the world.

Serving others is one way to witness.

Share your acrostics. Then pray together:

† God the Holy Spirit, give us the courage to be Jesus' witnesses.

Talk with your teacher about ways you and your family might use the "Faith Alive" section. Work with your family to decide how you will continue Jesus' mission. Then pray the prayer to the Holy Spirit.

REVIEW ▪ TEST

Answer the questions.

1. What is a Christian witness?

_____

_____

2. What happened at the Last Supper?

_____

_____

3. What happened on the feast of Pentecost?

_____

_____

4. How do we become members of the Church?

_____

_____

5. How will you show you are a member of Jesus' community, the Church today?

_____

_____

 **AT HOME AND IN THE PARISH**

 In this lesson your fourth grader learned how the Church began and what it means to belong to the Church today. The Holy Spirit guides and empowers the Church to continue the prophetic ministry of Jesus in every age. The Holy Spirit helps us today in the same way that the first Christians were helped to witness to their faith.

Your child has also learned that first of all we belong to the Church in our families.

Every family has the mission of witnessing to Christ, worshiping God, building community, sharing God's word, and serving as Jesus did.

†Prayer to the Holy Spirit
Invite your family to learn and pray this prayer together.

Come, Holy Spirit, fill the hearts of your faithful people and enkindle in us the fire of your love. Amen.

43

4 The Beatitudes

Lord, teach us to find true happiness in doing your will.

OUR LIFE

Once upon a time there was a very rich king called Midas. He was the richest man in the world, but he was not happy. He wanted more.

One day, as he sadly counted his gold, a stranger suddenly appeared before him. "Why are you sad, King Midas?" asked the stranger.

Midas said, "I wish everything I owned were gold."

"You shall have your wish," the stranger said.

The next morning when Midas awoke, he touched his blanket. It turned to gold! So did his clothes and his furniture! Midas was deliriously happy.

He had the golden touch! Suddenly his little daughter came running to him. She threw her arms around him and kissed him. She became a beautiful golden statue.

Finish the story and share your endings with one another. What do you think of Midas' wish and its results?

SHARING LIFE

If you could wish for something that would make you most happy, what would it be? Why?

Imagine what Jesus would wish for us. Share your ideas as a group.

Write your group's wishes in the first column of the treasure chest. Put Jesus' wishes for you in the second column.

HAPPINESS

Our Wish List	Jesus' Wish List for Us
Never be grounded or punished	*peace for all of us*

Compare the two lists. Circle any wish that shows up in both columns. Then think about what these lists tell you. This week we will be learning more about the meaning of true happiness.

We Will Learn

- The Beatitudes teach us how to be truly happy.

- When we live the Beatitudes, we become peacemakers.

- The Holy Spirit helps us live the Beatitudes.

45

- Begin by praying the Morning Offering together (page 291).

- Tell about some of the things that give you true happiness.

True Happiness

People sometimes think that having a lot of money or possessions or being famous will make them happy. Jesus taught that true happiness comes from doing God's loving will.

One day Jesus began to teach the people how to be truly happy, truly blessed. He taught them the Beatitudes.

Jesus said, "Blessed are the poor in spirit,
    for theirs is the kingdom of heaven" (Matthew 5:3).

The people were surprised. How was being poor going to make them happy? But being hungry or homeless was not the only kind of "poor" Jesus was talking about.

By being poor in spirit Jesus meant knowing that we depend on God for everything. We are poor in spirit when we know that we are always in need of God's help and ask him for it.

Then Jesus said,
"Blessed are they who mourn,
    for they will be comforted" (Matthew 5:4).

The mourning that Jesus was speaking about meant being sorry for sin, evil, and suffering in the world. We should remember that if we live as Jesus teaches, God will comfort us when we are in need.

Jesus also knew that some people had a false kind of pride. They thought that they had no need of God or other people. But Jesus said,
"Blessed are the meek,
    for they will inherit the land" (Matthew 5:5).

Humble people are gentle, kind, and patient with others. They do their good acts for God and not for the praise of other people.

Jesus understood that some people thought that if they always tried to be good, they would not have any fun. But Jesus said to them,
"Blessed are they who hunger and
    thirst for righteousness,
  for they will be satisfied"
(Matthew 5:6).

The **Beatitudes** are ways of living that Jesus gave us so that we can be truly happy.

This is difficult for us to understand.

Suppose your parent asks you to share your bike with your little brother or sister because there is no money to buy another.

You probably will not feel very happy at the moment. But when you see your sister's or brother's happiness, you will begin to understand.

Each time you say yes to God by being fair and just, you are doing God's loving will. This brings us true happiness.

Why do you think Jesus taught the Beatitudes?

Which of the Beatitudes do you think will be the easiest for you to live? the hardest? Why?

47

OUR CATHOLIC FAITH

- Jesus, help us to grow as just and peaceful people.

- Talk about times when you receive or give mercy.

The Beatitudes Bring Peace

Jesus continued teaching the people other Beatitudes, or ways to be truly happy and at peace. Jesus said, "Blessed are the merciful, for they
will be shown mercy" (Matthew 5:7).

Here Jesus is teaching us that it is not enough for us to be sorry for the wrong we have done. Jesus asks us to forgive everyone, people we do not like as well as our friends.

Jesus knew that many people spend their whole lives worrying. He told them not to worry but to trust in God instead. This is what Jesus meant when he said, "Blessed are the clean of heart,
for they will see God" (Matthew 5:8).

Being pure in heart means putting God first in our lives and doing his will.

In Jesus' time, just as today, the people longed for peace. Jesus said, "Blessed are the peacemakers,
for they will be called children of God" (Matthew 5:9).

Peace does not just happen. We must work for peace and reconciliation among people in our family, our school, our neighborhood, and our world.

Our Catholic bishops teach us that when we speak up for others who are being treated unfairly, we are peacemakers. We also bring peace to ourselves by making up, or being reconciled, with anyone with whom we are angry.

Finally, Jesus told the people that if they did God's will, they might be persecuted. Being persecuted can mean being made fun of, ignored or kept out of a group, or insulted. It can also mean being physically hurt, imprisoned, and even killed.

Jesus reminded us that there is a great reward for doing God's loving will. Jesus said,

"Blessed are those who are persecuted
    for the sake of righteousness,
  for theirs is the kingdom of heaven"
(Matthew 5:10).

The Beatitudes are the spirit of love, peace, justice, mercy, and generosity required of Jesus' disciples. They remind us that in living for God's kingdom, we find true happiness.

It is not easy to live the way of the Beatitudes. We need courage to live this way. But the Holy Spirit is with us and helps us live as Jesus' disciples.

"Blessed are the peacemakers,
  for they will be called children of God"
(Matthew 5:9).

Write what you will do right now to work for peace.

_____

_____

_____

_____

How can living the Beatitudes bring justice and peace to the world?

How will you be merciful this week? pure of heart?

OUR CATHOLIC FAITH

- Choose one Beatitude. In silence, ask Jesus to help you to live it.

- Explain why it takes courage for you to live the Beatitudes.

The Beatitudes in My Life

The Beatitudes	What They Mean
Blessed are the poor in spirit, for theirs is the kingdom of heaven.	People who are poor in spirit depend on God for everything. Nothing becomes more important than God.
Blessed are they who mourn, for they will be comforted.	People are saddened by sin, evil, and suffering in the world but trust that God will comfort them.
Blessed are the meek, for they will inherit the land.	Humble people show gentleness and patience toward others. They will share in God's promises.
Blessed are they who hunger and thirst for righteousness, for they will be satisfied.	People who are fair and just towards others are doing God's loving will.
Blessed are the merciful, for they will be shown mercy.	Merciful people are concerned about others' feelings. They are willing to forgive those who hurt them.
Blessed are the clean of heart, for they will see God.	People who keep God first in their lives are pure in heart. They give their worries and concerns to God.
Blessed are the peacemakers, for they will be called children of God.	Peacemakers are people who bring peace and reconciliation into the lives of others. They treat others fairly.
Blessed are those who are persecuted . . . , for theirs is the kingdom of heaven.	People who are willing to be ignored or insulted for doing what they feel God wants will share in his kingdom.

Matthew 5:3–10

Saint Anthony of Padua

What happens when we try to live the Beatitudes with courage? Eight hundred years ago, a boy was born in Portugal who would try to live the Beatitudes with courage. He became a saint. Little did he know as a young man that one day he would be thought of as one of the most popular saints of the Catholic Church. Today we call him Saint Anthony of Padua.

Even at an early age, Anthony's dream was to become a missionary. That is why he became a priest in the Franciscan Order. He was sent to do missionary work in northern Africa, but soon he had to return home because he got sick.

Anthony did not give up, however. He became a great teacher and preacher. Fearlessly, Anthony attacked the problems of his time. People who heard him speak were amazed at his courage and learning.

After a life of helping others to love God and to live the good news of Jesus, Anthony died at the age of 36 in Padua, Italy. He must have been a very holy person, because the Church declared him a saint just one year after his death.

Many parish churches have a statue or picture of Saint Anthony. The next time you see one, ask this holy saint to pray that you, too, might live the Beatitudes with courage. How can you be like Saint Anthony today?

Learn by heart Faith Summary

- The Beatitudes teach us how to follow Jesus and be truly happy.
- The Holy Spirit helps us to live the Beatitudes.
- The Beatitudes are the spirit of love, mercy, and generosity required of Jesus' disciples.

Coming to Faith

Do you think it takes courage to live with the spirit of love, peace, justice, mercy, and generosity that the Beatitudes teach? Explain.

Explain why you think Jesus calls these people "happy."

- the peacemakers
- the merciful
- those who work for justice

Practicing Faith

Form two teams. Each team will draw up eight "Who am I?" Beatitude questions. Each team will challenge the other to name the Beatitude. For example:

I call you to do what God wants even when people make fun of you or insult you. Who am I? (eighth Beatitude)

Pray together.

† Jesus, help us to be Beatitude people— people who work for peace, love, justice, mercy, and care for those in need. Then we will truly know the happiness of God's kingdom.

Close by reading aloud each Beatitude together slowly and prayerfully.

Talk with your teacher about ways you and your family might use the "Faith Alive" section. You might share the Beatitude prayer on this page with your family.

REVIEW ▪ TEST

Complete each Beatitude below.

1. Blessed are the _____, for
they will be shown mercy.

2. Blessed are those who mourn, for they will be

_____ .

3. Blessed are the poor in _____, for
theirs is the kingdom of heaven.

4. Blessed are the peacemakers, for they will be called

_____ of God.

5. How can you work for peace among your friends?

_____

_____

5 ‖ Living as Our Best Selves

Jesus, help us to remember that whatever we do for others, we do for you.

Our Life

One day Jesus told the parable of the Good Samaritan.

A man was traveling from Jerusalem to Jericho. Suddenly a gang attacked him, beat him badly, and took everything he had. They left him lying in a ditch, half dead.

Soon a priest from the Temple came along the road. He saw the man but walked by on the other side of the road. Then a Levite came by. He went over and looked at the man but then kept on going.

Finally a Samaritan, a foreigner and someone hated in Israel, came upon the man. He stopped, gently lifted the man and cared for his wounds. He put the man on his donkey and took him to an inn.

He gave the innkeeper money, saying, "Take care of him . . . I shall repay you on my way back."
See Luke 10:29-36

Which person do you think acted as a neighbor to the man?

What do you hear Jesus saying for your life?

Sharing Life

Did you ever help someone who didn't expect your help? Tell about it.

Who are some "good samaritans" in our world today?

Do you have to know someone in order to be a "neighbor" to them? Explain.

Work in small groups to create a "videostrip" (like the illustration on these pages) of a modern Good Samaritan story. Begin by asking yourselves:

- Who might be hurt or in need in our neighborhood, or school, or parish?

- Why might some people pass them by?

- Who might stop to help? What would the helpers do?

- How would your story end?

Share your "videostrips."

This week we will learn that we are all called to be good samaritans.

We Will Learn

- The Corporal Works of Mercy are ways we care for the physical needs of others.

- The Spiritual Works of Mercy are ways we care for the spiritual needs of others.

- As disciples of Jesus, Catholics live the Works of Mercy.

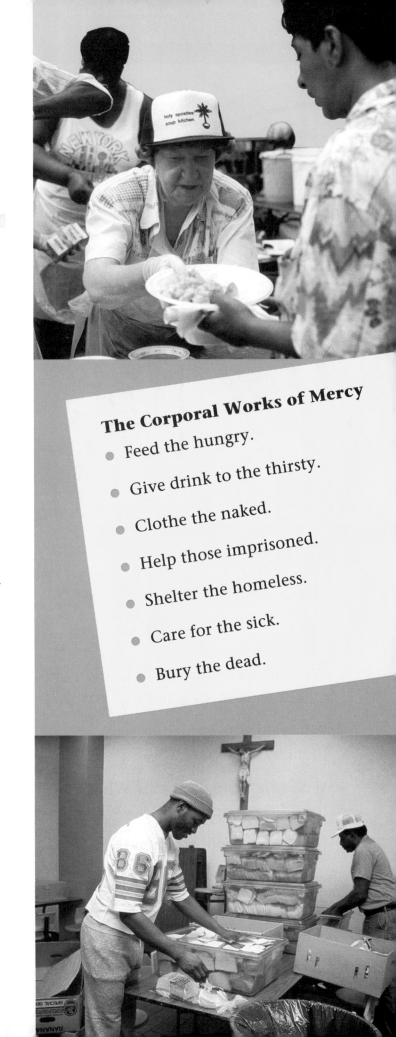

Jesus, our Brother, help us to find you in all our brothers and sisters.

What does "living the good news of Jesus" mean to you?

The Corporal Works of Mercy

The Catholic Church teaches us ways to help us care for the physical needs of others. They are called the Corporal Works of Mercy. *Corporal* refers to what our bodies need to be healthy and well.

Jesus taught his disciples how he wanted them to live. One day he told a large crowd that he would come again at the end of the world to judge everyone. At this last judgment, the Lord will separate people into two groups, just as a shepherd separates the sheep from the goats. To the first group on his right, he will say, "Come, you who are blessed by my Father. Inherit the kingdom prepared for you from the foundation of the world."

- I was hungry and you gave me food, thirsty and you gave me drink.

- I was a stranger and you welcomed me, naked and you clothed me.

- I was ill and you cared for me; in prison and you visited me.

The Corporal Works of Mercy

- Feed the hungry.
- Give drink to the thirsty.
- Clothe the naked.
- Help those imprisoned.
- Shelter the homeless.
- Care for the sick.
- Bury the dead.

Heaven is being with God and the friends of God forever.

These people will say, "Lord, when did we ever do any of these for you?"

Jesus will say, "I say to you, whatever you did for one of these least brothers of mine, you did it for me."

Then Jesus will turn to the other people and say, "Whenever you refused to help anyone, you refused to help me." Jesus will say to these people, "Depart from me!"

These people, "the goats," will be sent into the eternal punishment of hell. The others, "the sheep," who did God's will, shall receive eternal life with him in heaven.
Based on Matthew 25:31–46

When people are sick, lonely, without decent clothes, or hungry and homeless, they are not free to be happy. Jesus wants us to help set them free from their poverty and suffering.

- How did Jesus describe the end of the world? Explain.
- Learn the Corporal Works of Mercy by heart.

57

Jesus, help us to find you, love you, and serve you in others.

What more do you think we can do to answer the needs of others?

The Spiritual Works of Mercy

Sometimes people have problems that do not always show on the outside. People may be sad or confused. We say that they have spiritual needs.

To help us care for the spiritual needs of people, the Catholic Church teaches us the Spiritual Works of Mercy.

Sometimes people do not know about God or what he wants them to do. Jesus helped people to know and love God. We can do that, too.

When people are hurt or sad, they need to be comforted. Jesus always comforted people.

One time, Jesus looked over the city of Jerusalem. He said, "Jerusalem, Jerusalem, . . . how many times have I yearned to gather your children together . . . " (Matthew 23:37).

We, too, can comfort others.

The Spiritual Works of Mercy

- Share your knowledge with others.
- Give advice to those who need it.
- Comfort those who suffer.
- Be patient with people.
- Forgive those who hurt us.
- Give correction to those who need it.
- Pray for the living and the dead.

Jesus was patient with people. Many times his disciples did not understand the parables he told. Jesus would ask them, "Do you not understand this parable?" (Mark 4:13) Then he would patiently explain it again.

We, too, should have patience with others.

Jesus forgave all those who hurt him. On the cross, Jesus forgave those who crucified him. He said, "Father, forgive them, they know not what they do" (Luke 23:34).

Following Jesus' example, we can forgive others.

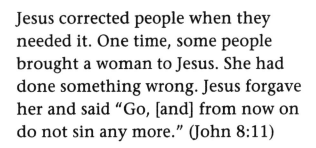

Jesus corrected people when they needed it. One time, some people brought a woman to Jesus. She had done something wrong. Jesus forgave her and said "Go, [and] from now on do not sin any more." (John 8:11)

We have to tell our friends who want to do wrong that we will not join them.

Jesus prayed all the time. He taught us how to pray. We need to pray each day for everyone, everywhere.

Choose and practice one Spiritual Work of Mercy today. Write what you will do.

_____

_____

_____

_____

_____

What are the Spiritual Works of Mercy?

Learn the Spiritual Works of Mercy by heart.

OUR CATHOLIC FAITH

Teach us, O God, to do the right and to love goodness and to walk humbly with you.

What do you think our community or world would be like if everyone practiced the Works of Mercy?

We Are Just and Merciful

Think how wonderful it would be if everyone had enough food and a decent place in which to live. How happy we would be if all who were sick or needed help had someone to care for them.

Then we would be living justly. Everyone would have a fair share. All people would have what they need to live happily.

How happy we would be if we were all patient, kind, and loving to one another. Then we would be living with mercy. We would be kind to one another, as God is kind to us.

If all of us were just and merciful, we would be living as God wants us to live. We would be living the way of the kingdom of God. We would be living life to the fullest.

Micah, a great prophet of justice and peace in the Old Testament, said: "You have been told . . .
    what the LORD requires of you:
Only to do the right and to love goodness
    and to walk humbly with your God."
(Micah 6:8).

To Bury the Dead

When Catholics look at the Works of Mercy, some wonder why burying the dead is included in the list. The answer is simple: Our bodies are temples of the Holy Spirit. For this reason, they must be treated with great care and reverence—both in life and in death.

Today Catholics show respect for someone who has died by attending a wake or vigil service the night before the funeral Mass. At the wake service, family and friends say prayers that remind them of their hope in God and in Christ's resurrection.

At the funeral Mass, the readings and music remind us again and again of the resurrection and of life forever with God. The Easter candle, a symbol of the risen Christ, is lit and placed near the coffin.

After the Mass, the coffin is taken to the cemetery where it is placed in blessed ground. This is done out of respect for the body, the temple of the Holy Spirit.

Listen closely to one of the prayers for the deceased used at the funeral Mass.

Make this prayer your own and remember to pray for all those who have died. In this way, you will be performing another work of mercy!

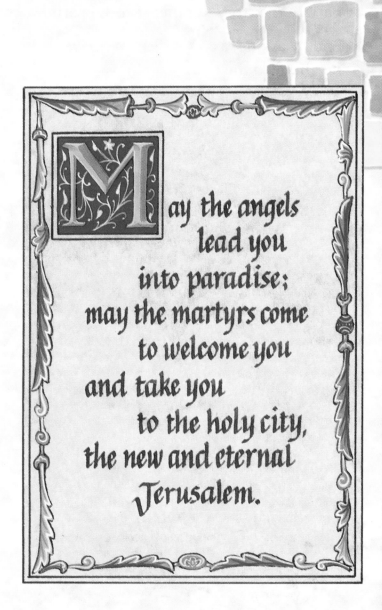

May the angels lead you into paradise; may the martyrs come to welcome you and take you to the holy city, the new and eternal Jerusalem.

Learn by heart **Faith Summary**

- The Corporal Works of Mercy are ways we care for one another's physical needs.

- The Spiritual Works of Mercy are ways we care for one another's spiritual needs.

- As disciples of Jesus, we must live the Corporal and Spiritual Works of Mercy.

COMING TO FAITH

Have one group act out the story of the Good Samaritan. Choose someone to narrate the story as others act the parts.

End by asking, as Jesus did, "Who was neighbor to the man?"

Then have another group act out Jesus' story of the last judgment.

Ask one another: Why is it Jesus himself for whom we are caring when we do the works of mercy?

PRACTICING FAITH

Talk with a friend about one way you can practice a work of mercy this week.

Decide when and how you will do it. Share your decision with the group.

End by praying the Family Prayer as a group.

Talk with your teacher about ways you and your family might use the "Faith Alive" section. Ask your family to help you live one of the Works of Mercy this week.

REVIEW ■ TEST

Circle the letter beside the correct answer.

1. The _____ Works of Mercy help us care for the physical needs of others.

    a. Spiritual   **b.** Heavenly   **c.** Corporal

2. When we help someone who is sad, we are doing a _____ Work of Mercy.

    a. Spiritual   **b.** Corporal   **c.** Divine

3. _____ is being with God and the friends of God forever.

    a. Mercy   **b.** Church   **c.** Heaven

4. Jesus said, "Whatever you did for one of these least brothers of mine, you did it for _____."

    a. me."   **b.** nothing."   **c.** love."

5. Write one way you will try to live justly.

_____

_____

FAITH ALIVE AT HOME AND IN THE PARISH

In this chapter your fourth grader learned that Jesus taught us how we will be judged as his disciples. Jesus was never stronger in his teaching than when he spoke about the ways we must care for others. The beautiful parable of the Good Samaritan and the parable of the Last Judgment make clear what our responsibilities are in living our Catholic faith. As a family, help one another to see that the Corporal and Spiritual Works of Mercy are ways to live for the reign of God. See how well your child can explain them to you. Talk about their importance for your family and about ways the Church helps us to practice them.

Living the Law of Love

The Works of Mercy are ways we live the Law of Love. Ask your child to tell you what the Law of Love is. Then look around your neighborhood and see which people need love and care. Talk with your child about ways your family can try to help these people. Then choose something you will do.

†Family Prayer

Close your eyes.
Picture Jesus talking to you.
In your own words, tell Jesus how you want to live the Works of Mercy.
Ask Jesus for his help.

6 | Celebrating Reconciliation

Jesus, teach us how to forgive and how to be forgiven.

Our Life

One day Jesus was teaching the people in a friend's house. There was a paralyzed man who wanted Jesus to heal him. His friends carried him to the house but because of the crowds they could not get near. So they carried the paralytic to the roof, opened up some tiles, and lowered the man on his mat right down in front of Jesus. Jesus smiled. He was pleased with the man's faith. He said, "Your sins are forgiven".

The teachers of the Law were horrified. "Who is this who speaks blasphemies? Who but God alone can forgive sins?

Jesus looked at them. "Which is easier," he said, "to say 'Your sins are forgiven,' or to say 'Rise and walk'? But that you may know that the Son of Man has authority on earth to forgive sins." Jesus turned to the paralyzed man and said, "Rise, pick up your stretcher, and go home."

All at once the man got up and went home rejoicing and praising God.
Based on Luke 5:17–26

Why did Jesus both forgive the paralytic's sins and help him to walk again?

How does it feel to be truly forgiven?

Sharing Life

Imagine that you are the paralyzed man. Your friends lower you right in front of Jesus. He smiles at you. He is pleased that you trust him so much. How do you feel when:

- he says you are forgiven?

- he tells you to walk?

- you realize you are both forgiven and cured?

64

Here are some everyday situations in which one person is wronged and the other must seek reconciliation. Choose a situation to act out with a partner.

This activity might help us examine more closely our need for reconciliation.

After each role-play, talk about the way each situation was settled. How was reconciliation achieved?

This week we will learn more about the sacrament of Reconciliation.

- A friend who promises to meet you at the library never shows up.

- You borrow a friend's tape and carelessly record over it.

We Will Learn

- Sometimes we do not live for God's kingdom. We sin.

- We prepare for the sacrament of Reconciliation.

- We take part in a prayer service of reconciliation.

- Your friend is being made fun of; you say nothing.

65

God Always Forgives

As disciples of Jesus Christ, we are called to love and care for one another. We are to live for God's kingdom of justice and peace for all people.

When we live as Jesus taught, we help everyone to know that God is with us now. But we do not always live for God's kingdom or do what he wants us to do. We do not always love God and others as we should. We do not always love ourselves in the right way. Sometimes we sin. We sin when we freely choose to do something that we know is wrong. We disobey God's law on purpose.

God always forgives us if we are sorry and show it. We want the person we have hurt to forgive us. We want God to forgive us, too. We celebrate his forgiveness in the sacrament of Reconciliation.

Preparing for Reconciliation

We prepare for the sacrament of Reconciliation by thanking God for having loved us so much and by examining our conscience. We think about the Ten Commandments, the Law of Love, and the Beatitudes. We ask ourselves whether we have been living the way that Jesus showed us to live. (See pages 80, 81, and 50.)

We think about the Corporal Works of Mercy and ask ourselves whether we have been caring for people's physical needs. We think about the Spiritual Works of Mercy and ask ourselves whether we have been caring for the spiritual needs of others. (You can review these on pages 56 and 58.)

We think of the good things we have done and thank God. We ask God to help us to continue living as disciples of Jesus for the kingdom of God.

I'M SORRY

I'M SORR

We think of the good things that we could have done, but did not do. We decide that we will try harder to live for God's kingdom.

We think of the sinful things we may have done. We tell God we are sorry. We promise to try to change our lives and we ask for God's help. We remember to tell the person whom we might have hurt that we are sorry, too.

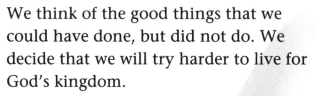

COMING TO FAITH

Take a few minutes now to think about the ways you have tried to live as a follower of Jesus Christ.

Try to shut out any noises or distractions. Ask yourself how you have tried to do God's loving will by the way you have lived this week.

Thank God for the good things you have done. Ask God to forgive your sins and failings and to help you do better. Now let's pray together.

67

PRACTICING FAITH

A Prayer Service for Forgiveness

Opening Hymn

Joyful, joyful, we adore you,
God of glory, Lord of love;
Hearts unfold like flowers before you,
Opening to the sun above.
Melt the clouds of sin and sadness;
Drive the dark of doubt away;
Giver of eternal gladness,
Fill us with the light of day.

Reader: (Read Matthew 25:31–45.)

(Pause for silent reflection on reading.)

Prayer Response

Leader: For failing to be aware that God is with us in our lives,

All: Jesus, we ask for forgiveness.

Leader: For the times we choose not to live for God's kingdom,

All: Jesus, we ask for forgiveness.

Leader: For the times when we did not care for the needs of others,

All: Jesus, we ask for forgiveness.

Leader: For the times when we did not care for people who are hungry,

All: Jesus, we ask for forgiveness.

Leader: For the times we were not peacemakers,

All: Jesus, we ask for forgiveness.

All: (Pray the Our Father together.)

Leader: Let us exchange a sign of peace with one another.

Closing Hymn

Sing to the tune of "Joyful, Joyful!"

Jesus, Jesus please forgive us,
For the times we did not love.
We will try to be disciples,
And spread peace and joy to all.
Thank you, God, for your forgiveness
For our failings and our sins.
We are joyful for God's blessings,
Helping us to love again.

Talk with your teacher about ways you and your family can use the "Faith Alive" section. Discuss with a family member ways to prepare to celebrate the sacrament of Reconciliation.

REVIEW ∙ TEST

Answer the questions.

1. In the gospel account of the paralyzed man, Jesus did two things for the man. What are they?

forgived him

healed him

2. What is sin?

It is when a person is bad

3. In what sacrament do we celebrate God's forgiveness?

reconciliation

4. What things should we think of when examining our conscience? Name at least two.

sins and good things we have done

5. How does Reconciliation help you to grow as a disciple of Jesus?

to believe in Jesus

FAITH ALIVE AT HOME AND IN THE PARISH

In this chapter your fourth grader was reminded about the way God wants us to live as disciples of Jesus and about the gift of the sacrament of Reconciliation. It is important that we help our children understand the connection between reconciliation and conversion. Conversion is a lifelong process of turning *away* from sin and turning *toward* God. Reconciliation heals us and strengthens us to continue our journey toward God. It involves both trying not to sin again and making up with those whom our sins have hurt.

Learn by heart **Faith Summary**

- We sin when we freely choose to do what we know is wrong. We disobey God's law on purpose.

- God always forgives us when we are sorry.

- We examine our conscience to prepare for Reconciliation.

7 Celebrating Eucharist

Jesus, may the Eucharist help us to share our lives with others.

OUR LIFE

Special Friends: A Play

Anna: Mrs. Carr, what a great trip to the community center! It was like spending the day with my grandparents. Everyone was so friendly.

Mrs. Carr: It seems like we all enjoyed the day. How about if we take turns to share what we remember.

Mike: Mr. Ricco is a good story teller. His stories about the war made me feel I was right there with him.

Chris: Everyone really liked our sandwiches and cookies! Mrs. Beltmen told me we should get the golden apron award.

Ashley: Did you see how Mr. Drake carved a face in my apple? It looked so real I didn't want to ruin it by eating it.

Mrs. Carr: Do you remember the song all our new friends sang before we ate our lunch? Let's sing it together.

Jerome: Oh, I remember it! Mrs. Foster played it on the piano. She said it was the same tune as "She'll Be Coming 'Round the Mountain."

All: Let us show that we are grateful
for God's gifts.
Let us show that we are grateful
for God's gifts.
Let us praise our God in heaven.
Let us all sing our thanksgiving.
Let us show that we are grateful
for God's gifts.

What have you learned from senior citizens you know?

How do you show your thanks for older people?

SHARING LIFE

Imagine Jesus came to share a meal with us. What would we talk to him about?

Do you think Jesus is with you when you share with others? How?

Work in a small group. See whether you can write a second verse to the song "Let Us Show We are Grateful." In this new verse, focus on the idea that the Eucharist calls us to be caring people— for example, to be "bread" for others.

Share and sing your verses together as a way to enter into this lesson.

This week we will learn more about the celebration of the Eucharist.

We Will Learn

● The Eucharist is our greatest prayer of praise and thanks to God.

● We are united with one another and with Jesus Christ when we receive Holy Communion.

OUR CATHOLIC FAITH

The Eucharist

Jesus Christ is with us today in a special way in the Eucharist. We celebrate the Eucharist at Mass, our greatest prayer of praise and thanks to God. The Mass is both a meal and a sacrifice. Together as a parish family, we gather as a worshiping assembly for the celebration of Mass.

At Mass we remember all that Jesus did to save us. At the Last Supper, on the night before he died, Jesus celebrated the feast of Passover with his friends.

During the meal, Jesus took bread and gave thanks to God. He gave the bread to his friends and said, "Take this, all of you, and eat it; this is my body, which will be given up for you."

Then he took a cup of wine and gave thanks to God. He gave the cup to his disciples and said, "Take this, all of you, and drink from it: this is the cup of my blood, the blood of the new and everlasting covenant. It will be shed for you and for all so that sins may be forgiven."

The bread and wine were now the Body and Blood of Jesus, even though they still looked and tasted like bread and wine. Jesus told his friends, "Do this in memory of me."

Jesus showed us how much he loved us by giving us this wonderful gift of himself in Holy Communion. When we celebrate the Mass, we thank God that Jesus is really with us. Jesus promised his disciples that he would never leave them. Jesus said, "I am with you always, until the end of the age" (Matthew 28:20).

The Last Supper, **Phillipe de Champaigne, circa 1648**

We Celebrate the Eucharist

In the Liturgy of the Word, we come together as an assembly of faith. We listen to the Bible readings to hear what God is saying to us today. We pray a psalm and proclaim our faith. We ask God to help us.

In the Liturgy of the Eucharist, we give thanks to God and offer him gifts of bread and wine. Through the power of the Holy Spirit and the words and actions of the priest, our gifts become the Body and Blood of Christ.

The priest breaks the consecrated Host. This reminds us that we all receive the one Bread of Life in Holy Communion. We know that we are united with one another in Jesus Christ when we share his Body and Blood in Holy Communion. Jesus is with us. We tell him what is in our hearts.

Learn and pray together the "Holy, Holy, Holy" that we pray at Mass. (See page 291.)

COMING TO FAITH

Tell in your words what Jesus did at the Last Supper.

What can you say to Jesus the next time you receive Him in Holy Communion?
Write your prayer below.

† Dear Jesus,

_____

_____

_____

_____

_____

_____

73

PRACTICING FAITH

Preparing a Mass

Divide into small groups. Review the parts of the Mass. Write down the plan for your group Mass.

Theme: Ask your catechist to help you find the readings in the Lectionary for the Mass. Read them and decide together the theme of this Mass.

Introductory Rites

Hymn: Choose an opening hymn.

_____

Liturgy of the Word

Readings: Choose people to read the two readings from the Bible and the psalm response.

Old Testament reading:

Book, Chapter, Verses

_____

Reader: _____

Psalm and New Testament reading:

Psalm Response

_____

Book, Chapter, Verses

_____

Reader: _____

Prayer of the Faithful: Write several petitions to use at Mass.

_____

_____

Liturgy of the Eucharist

Presentation of Gifts: Decide who will bring up the plate or ciborium, which contains the altar breads, and the wine and water.

Bread _____

Wine _____

Water _____

Concluding Rite

Hymn: Choose a hymn of thanksgiving.

_____

Talk with your teacher about ways you and your family might use the "Faith Alive" section. As a family, you might want to make a list of people who need your prayers.

REVIEW ■ TEST

Answer the questions.

1. What is the Mass?

_____

_____

2. What is Holy Communion?

_____

3. What do we do during the Liturgy of the Word?

_____

_____

4. At what part of the Mass do we offer gifts of bread and wine to God?

_____

5. Does the Eucharist make a difference in your life? Explain.

_____

_____

FAITH ALIVE AT HOME AND IN THE PARISH

In this chapter your fourth grader was reminded of the meaning of the Eucharist and its central importance in the lives of Catholics. The Eucharist has been a central mystery of our faith from the earliest days of the Church. We read in the Acts of the Apostles that the early Christians "devoted themselves to the teaching of the apostles and to the communal life, to the breaking of the bread and to the prayers" (Acts 2:42). They also held all goods and property in common and provided for each member according to need. For them, the Eucharist was the source and summit of their lives.

Sharing in the Eucharist was an extension of a life shared in mutual concern and service. The same is true of our faith community today.

Learn by heart **Faith Summary**

- Jesus is really present in the Eucharist.

- The Eucharist is our greatest prayer of praise and thanksgiving to God.

- We share the Body and Blood of Christ in Holy Communion.

75

8 | Living as God's People

O God, your law is good. It gives us strength and guidance.

OUR LIFE

Grandmother was going to drive the twins to the community's baseball game. "Please put your seat belts on," the twins' grandmother said. "It is the law when people ride in a car."

"That's a silly law," Brian said.

"I don't want to be strapped in. I like to move around," Marcia added.

The twins were not happy, but they did not want to be late for the game. So they did what their grandmother wanted and obeyed the law. They had only driven a few blocks when their car was hit by another car that had run a red light. The police officer said they were lucky not to be seriously injured. "Your seat belts saved your lives," he said.

What are some laws that you follow each day? Make a list together.

How does each law help us?

SHARING LIFE

Does God have rules and laws for us to follow? What are they?

Why does God give us laws to live by?

Imagine what would happen in our lives without good laws. Tell about it.

Work with a partner and role-play what life might be like without good laws. Here are some ideas.

What if there were no laws about . . .

- dumping garbage any place people wanted
- destroying property
- stopping at a red light
- selling drugs
- using guns
- stealing

Share and discuss your ideas to help you prepare for what we will learn about God's laws.

We Will Learn

- God gave Moses the Ten Commandments.
- The Ten Commandments help us to live with true freedom.
- The Ten Commandments help us to live the Law of Love.

**OUR CATHOLIC FAITH**

■ Dear God, we love you more than anything else in the world.

■ What kind of laws do we need to live as God's people?

The Ten Commandments

God wants all people to love one another and to love him. But God does not force us to love. God wants people to be free to love him, to love one another, and to love themselves. Living the Law of Love, as Jesus taught us, helps us to be truly free.

In the Bible we read about the Israelites, God's chosen people. In ancient times they spent many years as slaves in Egypt. But God wanted them to be free and rescued them from slavery.

One day, God spoke to an Israelite named Moses. God told him to tell the people of Israel, "I am the Lord. I will free you . . . I will rescue you . . . ."

See Exodus 6:6

God chose Moses to lead the Israelites out of Egypt to freedom. Once free, they came to a place called Mount Sinai. Then Moses went up the mountain, where God made a covenant, or agreement, with the people. God told Moses to tell the people, "If you hearken to my voice and keep my covenant, you shall be my special possession, dearer to me than all other people." (Exodus 19:5).

A covenant is an agreement between God and people. In a covenant both sides make a special promise. God promised to protect the Israelites and help them to live in freedom. The Israelites promised to follow God's loving will and live as his own people.

FAITH WORD

The **Ten Commandments** are laws given to us by God to help us live as God's people.

Then God gave Moses special commandments, or laws, that would help the people keep their covenant with God and live in peace with one another. We call them the Ten Commandments. Living the Ten Commandments would help the Israelites to remain free as God's own people.

When Moses came down from the mountain, he told the Israelites that God had given them the commandments. The Israelites knew that by living these commandments they would keep their covenant with God and live in the freedom that he wanted for them. The people said to Moses, "All that the Lord has said, we will heed and do." Exodus 24:7

God wants us to live as his own people. We must obey God's commandments if we are to live together in peace and happiness. Keeping the laws of God brings us true freedom.

- Tell the story of God giving the Ten Commandments.

- Do you want to live in true freedom? How will the Ten Commandments help you?

OUR CATHOLIC FAITH

- Begin by praying Glory to the Father together. (See page 290.)

- Explain what it means to you to be truly free.

The Commandments and Us

God makes a special covenant with us at our Baptism. As Christians, we, too, are God's own people. God promises to be with us always to love and help us. We promise to obey the Ten Commandments. We promise to live as disciples of Jesus by living the Law of Love.

The Ten Commandments are God's laws for us today. They help us to live with true freedom as God's people. When we follow the Ten Commandments, we show that we belong to God and that we put him first in our lives. We say yes to God's covenant by living responsibly. Doing God's loving will is our best way to live in true freedom.

The Ten Commandments are laws for living with the freedom that God wants us to have. They help us to live the Law of Love, which Jesus taught.

THE TEN COMMANDMENTS

1. I, the LORD, am your God, who brought you out . . . that place of slavery. You shall not have other gods besides me.

2. You shall not take the name of the LORD, your God, in vain.

3. Remember to keep holy the Sabbath day.

4. Honor your father and your mother.

5. You shall not kill.

6. You shall not commit adultery.

7. You shall not steal.

8. You shall not bear false witness against your neighbor.

9. You shall not covet your neighbor's wife.

10. You shall not covet your neighbor's house.

See Exodus 20 and Deuteronomy 5

THE LAW OF LOVE

The first three commandments help us to love and honor God.

The Law of Love tells us, "Love the Lord, your God, with all your heart, with all your being, with all your strength, and with all your mind."

The last seven commandments help us to love others and ourselves.

The Law of Love tells us, "Love . . . your neighbor as yourself."

Based on Luke 10:27

Choose and write one of the commandments. Tell how you will try to live it right now.

_____

_____

_____

_____

_____

Learn the Ten Commandments by heart.

How will you try to put God first in your life this week?

OUR CATHOLIC FAITH

- Begin by praying together Psalm 19 on this page.

- Why do you think God gives us laws to live by?

Living as God's People

Obeying the first three commandments helps us to love God. This is the first part of the Law of Love.

Obeying the last seven commandments helps us to live the second part of the Law of Love, to love our neighbor as we love ourselves.

This will only happen if we freely choose to obey the Ten Commandments. We obey them out of love for God, not only out of fear of punishment. When we obey out of love, we know the peace that comes from doing God's loving will.

The Ten Commandments help us to do God's will and to live for the kingdom of God. They can help us to grow strong, wise, and happy in our lives as Catholic Christians.

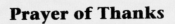

Prayer of Thanks

Today, Jews as well as Christians pray the following prayer of thanks to God for the Ten Commandments.

The law of the LORD is perfect,
   refreshing the soul.
The decree of the LORD is trustworthy,
   giving wisdom to the simple. . . .
The command of the LORD is clear,
   enlightening the eye. . . .
The statutes of the LORD are true,
   all of them just.

Psalm 19:8–10

Can Laws Change?

The Ten Commandments are laws that can never be changed. This is because they are God's laws, and God wants us to obey them all our lives.

There are some laws, however, that do change. We call these *human laws*. Human laws can be made by the government or by the Church. They are made to help people for a certain time in history.

People in your family may remember when Catholics who wanted to receive Holy Communion had to fast from food and liquid—including water—from midnight. But as parish Mass schedules and people's working schedules changed, the Church decided to change the law. Now we are required to fast for only one hour before receiving Communion.

This change was made to encourage Catholics to receive Holy Communion more frequently.

All laws are important. The Church guides us in understanding which laws are God's laws and which laws are human laws. Take time to ask your grandparents or other adults about Church laws that have changed during their lifetime.

Learn by heart Faith Summary

- God gave Moses the Ten Commandments to give to the people.

- The Ten Commandments help us to live with true freedom as God's people.

- The Ten Commandments help us to live the Law of Love, which Jesus taught.

COMING TO FAITH

Make a set of cards with these key words as shown. Divide into two teams. Choose captains. The captain of each team will, in turn, choose a card and ask a member of the opposite team to tell everything he or she knows about the word. Your teacher will be the judge and rate the response: 3 (fantastic), 2 (okay), or 1 (keep working).

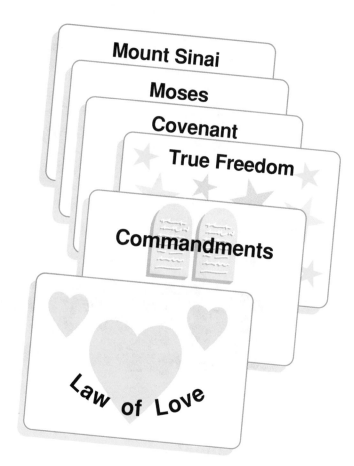

PRACTICING FAITH

God has made a covenant with us. We, on our part, have made a covenant with God to keep the commandments and live as God's people.

Work together to draw up your own "group covenant" with God for this year. Choose something special to do together to show you are God's people.

Plan your ideas here. Share them. Then write down the "group covenant." When it is completed, have someone read it aloud to the group. Then pray together the Our Father.

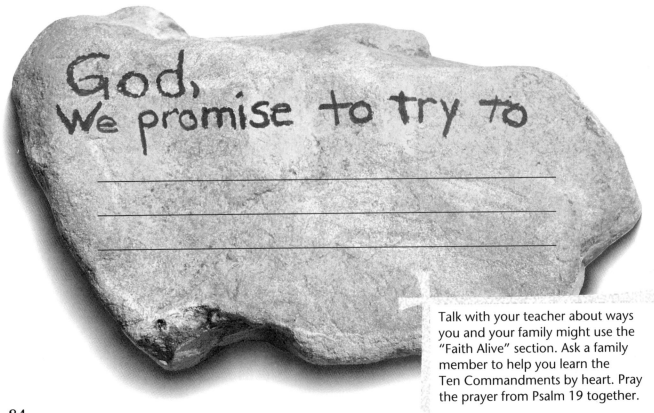

God, We promise to try to

_____

_____

_____

Talk with your teacher about ways you and your family might use the "Faith Alive" section. Ask a family member to help you learn the Ten Commandments by heart. Pray the prayer from Psalm 19 together.

REVIEW ■ TEST

Match.

1. Third Commandment   _____ You shall not kill.

2. Fifth Commandment   _____ You shall not tell lies
against your neighbor.

3. Eighth Commandment   _____ Honor your father and mother.

4. Fourth Commandment   _____ You shall not steal.

_____ Remember to keep holy
the Sabbath day.

5. Write one way you will live the second commandment.

_____

_____

FAITH ALIVE AT HOME AND IN THE PARISH

In this chapter your fourth grader learned that the Ten Commandments teach us how to do God's loving will. Before God gave the Israelites the commandments, he reminded them about who it was that had set them free. God gives us the Ten Commandments to help us live in true freedom and to grow strong, wise, and happy in our lives as Catholics.

Go over the Ten Commandments with your family. Talk about the reasons why God gave them to us. Discuss the fact that for each person some commandments are harder to keep than others. Then share ways we can support one another in obeying all the commandments.

A Ten Commandments Mobile

Cut out a daisy with ten petals. Together, write a commandment on each petal and attach it to a center circle labeled "The Ten Commandments." On the back of each petal write a brief statement about the meaning of the commandment. Color all the petals. Hang the daisy where it can be seen. This week take time to review each of the petals with your child.

9 Living as Free People

Junk food/Healthy food ?

Study/Cheat ?

?Chores/T.V. ?

OUR LIFE

Our lives are full of decisions and choices to be made. Some are so simple that they hardly need too much attention. For example, it does not require much decision making to choose to wear shoes or sneakers to school.

We need to think through other decisions more carefully. This is because some decisions we make may not be good for us. For example: If I am offered a cigarette and choose to smoke it, this decision will affect my health.

Take a few minutes to write on a small piece of paper an important choice someone your age might have to make. Fold your paper and put all the papers in a box.

SHARING LIFE

One by one, take a paper from the box. Read the "choice" to the group and share what you think the responsible decision should be.

What things do we think about when making a good decision?

Talk together and share your ideas.

Work in a small group. Your group will select one of the choices discussed. Talk it over, then enter it on the chart.

Share your charts with the whole group.

Decision Chart

Choice	Decision	Why	Consequences
To smoke or not to smoke	Not to smoke	It will harm my health and that of others. God wants me to care for my body.	I will have a much healthier life.

This week we will learn more about the way Christians make good decisions.

We Will Learn

- We are responsible for our choices.
- We can sin by what we choose to do.
- We can sin by what we fail to do, or do not do.

OUR CATHOLIC FAITH

Adam and Eve not only hurt themselves by their sin. They also hurt all their decendants. This means that every person born into the world suffers because of the sin of our first parents. This is what we mean by original sin.

○ O God, teach us to do your loving will.

○ What choices do you find easy to make? difficult? Why?

Making Choices

Some choices are easy; others are difficult. They are difficult because it often seems easier to do the wrong thing. Sometimes others—even young people our own age—will make fun of us for doing the right thing.

God has given us a free will. This means we can choose between right and wrong. We are responsible for saying yes or no to God.

God created us free to think, to choose, and to love. We are free to be faithful to God and to live according to his loving will for us. But people do not always choose to do God's will.

At the very beginning of human history, Adam and Eve chose to turn away from God. They lost the holiness God had given them. Through them, sin and evil came into the world.

Because of original sin, we have been weakened. That's why it is sometimes dificult for us to avoid sin.

All of us have to make many difficult choices in our lives. We need help and guidance. Catholics turn to the community of the Church for this guidance.

Think of a difficult choice you have to make. Write a prayer to the Holy Spirit for courage to choose wisely.

_____

_____

_____

_____

_____

To make difficult choices, we need to:

- take time to think over what we are about to do.
- ask the Holy Spirit to guide us and give us courage to make the right choice.
- remember the teachings of our Catholic faith.
- look at all the choices.
- see which choices will show that we love God and others.
- say no to the choices that will hurt us, others, or God's creation.
- choose to do the right thing.
- go to others for help when it is hard to do the right thing.

 Together go over the steps used in making a good choice.

Share how you will try to make responsible choices today.

OUR CATHOLIC FAITH

- Begin by praying the Our Father together.

- Talk together about what it means to commit a sin. Why do we sometimes sin?

Sinning by What We Do

Jesus came to show us how to choose to love God, others, and ourselves. But sometimes we choose to turn away from God. We sin. Sin is freely choosing to do what we know is wrong. When we sin, we disobey God's law on purpose.

Some people think that when they do the wrong thing by mistake, they have sinned. Everyone makes mistakes. For example, we often say or do something that we did not intend. Mistakes are not sins.

Temptations also are not sins. We may feel like stealing something. But if we choose not to steal, we have not given in to the temptation. We have not sinned.

The Catholic Church teaches us that we can sin in thought, word, or action. Some sins are so serious that by doing them we turn completely away from God's love. We call them mortal sins.

A sin is mortal when:

- what we do is very seriously wrong;

- we know that it is very wrong and that God forbids it;

- we freely choose to do it.

Some sins are less serious. We call them venial sins. We do not turn away completely from God's love but still hurt ourselves or others. We freely choose to be selfish.

All sins are personal choices. But sometimes whole groups of people can sin and hurt other people. We call this "social sin." When a group treats other people unjustly because of the color of their skin, or their age, or sex, or religion, it is a social sin.

Sin is never just between God and one person. Sin hurts us all. When we sin, we do not show love for God and his family. We care only for ourselves.

FAITH WORD

Sin is freely choosing to do what we know is wrong. When we sin, we disobey God's law on purpose.

If we want to be forgiven for any sin, we must be sorry for it. If we have hurt someone by our sin, we must try to make it up to that person. We must try to get rid of all forms of sin in our lives and in our society.

What is the difference among a mistake, a temptation, and a sin?

What must we do when we have sinned?

OUR CATHOLIC FAITH

- Begin by praying an Act of Contrition together. (See page 290.)

- Do you think we can sometimes sin by doing nothing at all? Explain.

Sinning by What We Do Not Do

We can also sin by what we do *not* do, as well as by what we choose to do. If someone is badly hurt or starving, and we choose not to give help, we may sin.

By standing by and doing nothing, we are choosing not to love as God commanded. By not reaching out in love to someone, we can be choosing to sin.

We can sin by not working for justice and peace for others. If people are being treated unfairly because of their age, race, sex, or religion, and we say or do nothing to help them, we can be choosing to sin.

God will always forgive us, no matter what we do, if we are truly sorry and try not to sin again. Ask the Holy Spirit to guide you and give you the courage always to make right choices.

No matter what questions or problems we face in life, we trust that the Holy Spirit will be with us. We also know that we can turn to the community of the Church for guidance and help.

Fifth Station: Simon helps Jesus carry His cross.

Stations of the Cross

Jesus Christ is the Savior of the world. Jesus is our Redeemer and Liberator. He saved, or freed, us from our sins. Jesus did this through his life, his death on the cross, and his resurrection.

For centuries, people have traveled to the Holy Land to follow in the footsteps of Jesus as he carried the cross to Calvary. Not everyone was able to make this journey, however. That is why Catholics began the custom of remembering Jesus' suffering and death by praying the stations of the cross.

The stations of the cross are fourteen pictures or carvings placed inside a parish church. These stations tell the story of Jesus as he traveled on his way to Calvary. They are called stations because the fourteen pictures are places where people stop and stand to remember and pray about the sufferings of Christ.

Praying the Stations

When we pray the stations, we begin with Pilate condemning Jesus to death, and we end with Jesus' burial in the tomb. Why not make a visit to your parish church to pray the stations of the cross? Stop at each station. Look at what is happening in each. Put yourself in the picture with Jesus. Then pray this prayer:

†We adore you, O Christ, and we praise you, because by your holy cross you have redeemed the world.

Learn by heart **Faith Summary**

- We can sin in thought, word, or action.

- Very serious sins are called mortal sins; less serious sins are called venial sins.

- A sin is mortal when what we do is very seriously wrong; we know that it is very wrong and that God forbids it; we freely choose to do it.

93

COMING TO FAITH

Are the people in the following situations making choices in keeping with God's will? Tell what you would say to them.

To belong to the "in" group at school Natalie has to join them in stealing from a store.

Your neighbors do not speak to the new family that has just moved in. They come from another country. What would you say to the new family? to your neighbors?

PRACTICING FAITH

Gather in a prayer circle. Imagine that Jesus is in the center of the circle. Be as still as you can and breathe silently in and out. Think of a difficult choice you have to make or might have to make. One by one stretch your arms out to the center. Imagine your hands are holding your choice. When everyone's arms are stretched out, pray together:

† Jesus, here are our choices. Help us to make decisions that are pleasing to you and helpful to us. We know that you will never leave us to face our difficulties alone. Amen.

Talk with your teacher about ways you and your family might use the "Faith Alive" section. Ask your family to share the peacemaking activity.

REVIEW ▪ TEST

Circle the letter beside the correct answer.

1. We sin when we

   a. freely choose to do wrong.   **b.** make mistakes.   **c.** are tempted.

2. God forgives our sins if we are

   a. in trouble because of them.   **b.** responsible for them.   **c.** sorry for them.

3. We call the first sin of the human race

   a. venial sin.   **b.** original sin.   **c.** serious sin.

4. Serious sins are called

   a. faults.   **b.** venial sins.   **c.** mortal sins.

5. As a Catholic, what should you do when you have an important decision to make?

_____

_____

FAITH ALIVE ▪ AT HOME AND IN THE PARISH

In this chapter your fourth grader learned that to live in true freedom, we must avoid sin. As disciples of Jesus and members of the Catholic Church, we must try to live according to God's law. Your child has learned that all sin is a personal choice. Very serious sin—one which completely separates us from God—is called mortal sin. Less serious sin is called venial sin. Sometimes we may even sin as a group of people or as a society. This is called social sin. As adults we also know how difficult it can be to do God's loving will and always to avoid sin. The Holy Spirit helps us make good moral choices, and the Church gives us the guidance we need.

Frequent examination of conscience is an excellent way to become more aware of the temptations we face and the choices we make every day. Encourage your child to make this practice a part of nightly prayer.

Making Peace at Home

As a family we experience many ups and downs. It is easy to celebrate our good moments. It is more difficult to celebrate our not-so-good moments. Plan a time for a "Making Peace Celebration"—perhaps before a meal. Invite each family member to think quietly of one thing for which he or she is sorry or wants to ask forgiveness. Then share a sign of peace.

10   God Is First in Our Lives
The First Commandment

God, we praise you! We give you glory! We put you first in our lives.

Our Life

The April weather was still unpredictable when Marty and his friend Steve decided to climb in the Rocky Mountains. Both young men were experienced climbers and moved easily up the face of the cliff.

They were almost to the top when clouds rolled in and the temperature dropped steadily. As Marty was swinging to a new foothold, his rope suddenly snapped. He fell ten feet to a ledge. Steve yelled that he would go for help. The injured Marty curled up on the ledge as snow fell and a cold wind lowered his body temperature. "I thought I was going to die there," he said. "I prayed and tried to stay awake."

Then morning came clear and cold. "The sun came up like fire," Marty recalls. "Even before I heard the shouts of the rescuers, I felt full of wonder and hope. I knew I was in God's hands."

When have you felt that God was really with you? Tell about it.

Sharing Life

What do you think it means to put God first in your life? What are some reasons for doing this? Share your thoughts as a group.

Now imagine that you are the stranded climber in this story or that you are in another dangerous situation. You are keeping a diary for four days.
Use the outline below.

Day 1
(What happened to you?)
_____
_____
_____
_____

Day 2
(How do you feel? Do you have hope? Is someone coming?)
_____
_____
_____
_____

Day 3
(Do you feel God is caring for you?)
_____
_____
_____
_____

Day 4
(What do you say to God?)
_____
_____
_____
_____
_____
_____

Share your diary with the group.

This week we will discover the place God should have in our lives.

We Will Learn

- The first commandment calls God's people to put God first in their lives.

- Jesus taught us and showed us how to put God first in our lives.

- We must choose to live the first commandment.

Our Catholic Faith

God of love, help us to love you with all our hearts, all our souls, all our strength.

What does it mean for you to put God first in your life?

The Israelites Put God First

When Moses gave the Ten Commandments of God to the people, he said, "Hear, O Israel! The LORD is our God, the LORD alone! Therefore, you shall love the LORD, your God, with all your heart, and with all your soul, and with all your strength. Take to heart these words which I enjoin on you today."

Deuteronomy 6:4–6

The Israelites trusted in God because they knew they were his people. They had a covenant with God and knew how much he loved them. Obeying God's commandments was the way they showed they were keeping their covenant with him.

The first commandment that Moses gave them was "I, the LORD, am your God, who brought you out of . . . that place of slavery. You shall not have other gods besides me" (Exodus 20:2–3).

This commandment was very important to the Israelites. They had been slaves of the Egyptians, but God rescued them from slavery and set them free. To remain free as God's people, the Israelites had to put him first in their lives.

When something in our life becomes more important than God, we are not free. We become slaves to it.

The Israelites put God first in their lives in many ways. They worshiped God in the Temple of Jerusalem. They studied the commandments in their synagogues. They prayed to God before and after every meal. What is most important, they put God first in their lives by trying to do his will—living with justice, peace, and love.

Sometimes the Israelites, like people today, found it hard to put God first in their lives. They discovered that it was the only way they could live in true freedom.

Today some people put things rather than God first in their lives. Instead of God, they think only of clothes or possessions or sports or being popular. They treat these things as if they were the most important things in their lives. They forget that only the one true God sets us free.

Why did the Israelites try to put God first in their lives?

How will you try to keep God first in your life today?

OUR CATHOLIC FAITH

- God of freedom, may your will be done on earth as it is in heaven.

- When do you find it hardest to put God first in your life?

Jesus Put God First

The first commandment tells us to keep God first in our lives, even when that is difficult. God knows that it is often hard for us to do this. Here is a Bible story showing that even Jesus was tempted not to obey the first commandment.

Jesus was led by the Holy Spirit into the desert. Jesus stayed there a long time. At the end of his stay in the desert, he was very hungry.

It was then that Jesus was tempted by the devil. The devil said to him, "If you are the Son of God, command this stone to become bread!"

Jesus answered, "It is written, 'One does not live by bread alone.'"

Then the devil showed Jesus all the kingdoms of the world. The devil told him, "I shall give to you all this power and their glory . . . if you worship me."

Jesus answered, "It is written, 'You shall worship the Lord, your God, and him alone shall you serve.'"

Then the devil took Jesus to Jersusalem and stood him on the highest point of the Temple. He said to Jesus, "If you are the Son of God, throw yourself down from here . . . ."

As disciples of Jesus, we look to him to show us how to put God first in our lives. One way Jesus did this was to spend time in prayer. When we read the gospels, we see that Jesus often prayed alone; he often prayed with his disciples, too. Jesus teaches us that to be able to obey any of God's commandments, we must be people of prayer.

Jesus also gave us the Church, guided by the Holy Spirit, to help us keep God first in our lives. In the Church, we grow in our relationship with God, and we come to know the one true God: Father, Son, and Holy Spirit.

Our lives should be centered on the one true God, the God who has loved us first. Today some people are tempted to make "false gods" out of clothes, food, being famous, possessions—even other people. We may be tempted to think that something is more important than God. But when God is most important in our lives, we are obeying the first commandment and showing how much we love God. We are also following Jesus' example. In this way we can bring about God's kingdom of justice and peace for all.

By obeying the first commandment, we help God's kingdom to come. We live in the freedom that only God can give.

Jesus answered, "It also says, 'You shall not put the Lord, your God, to the test.'"
Based on Luke 4:1–12

Then the devil left Jesus. He could not get Jesus to disobey the first commandment. Jesus did not give in to any of the devil's temptations. Jesus always put the Father first in his life.

■ Name the three ways that Jesus was tempted by the devil.

■ How will you try to follow Jesus' example of saying no to sin?

OUR CATHOLIC FAITH

Merciful God, lead us not into temptation but deliver us from evil. Amen.

What happens when God is most important in your life?

Choosing to Put God First

The first commandment tells us to worship God as the one true God. Sometimes people choose to put their faith in things or other people, and not in God. They believe in all kinds of magic and superstitions. They have more faith in horoscopes and fortune-tellers than they have in God.

Living by the first commandment means that we put all our faith in God and choose to keep him first in our lives.

When God is most important in our lives, we live in freedom and work to bring about God's kingdom, or reign, of justice and peace for all.

When we obey the first commandment, we never have to fear the future or put our trust in magic or chance. God's love and care for us is greater than anyone can imagine.

We should also remember to pray for those who do not believe in God or put their trust in God. By our prayers and good example, someday these people may come to know the one true God.

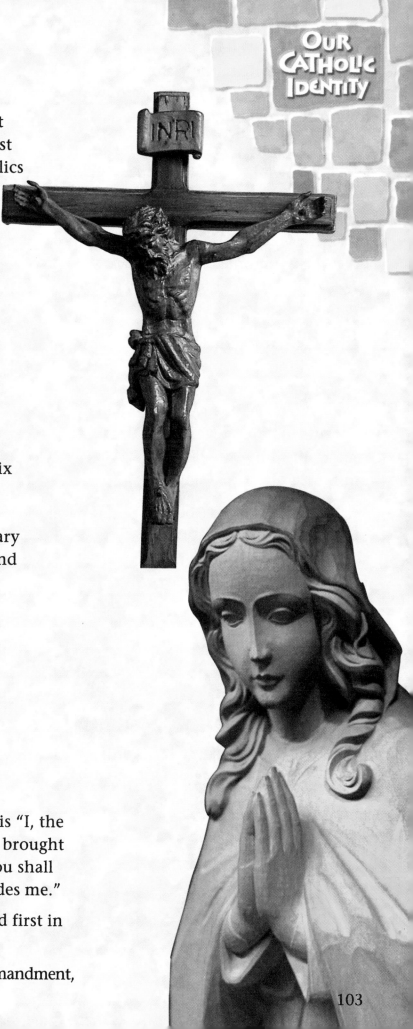

Statues and Crucifixes

Some people wonder why Catholics have statues and crucifixes in their homes and churches. They think that having crucifixes and statues is against the first commandment—that Catholics are adoring images. But Catholics do not worship images. We use them only to turn our minds and hearts to God in prayer. We worship God alone.

Catholics use the crucifix to remind us of Jesus and all that he did for us. We use statues of the Blessed Virgin Mary and the other saints to remind us of their holy lives and to ask them to pray for us.

Many Catholic families place a crucifix in a bedroom or another room of the house. Another Catholic custom is to have a statue of the Blessed Virgin Mary or one of the saints, or some other kind of religious art, in our homes. Good religious art helps us to pray and reminds us to live as Jesus' disciples.

What religious art would you like to choose? What will it help you to remember?

Learn by heart **Faith Summary**

- The first commandment is "I, the LORD, am your God, who brought you out of . . . slavery. You shall not have other gods besides me."

- Jesus taught us to put God first in our lives.

- When we live the first commandment, we live in true freedom.

103

COMING TO FAITH

Create an ending to these stories to show how each person chooses to live the first commandment.

Angie has a very large paper route and earns her own money. The paper route takes all her free time after school. She has no time to do her homework or to play with her friends. Her family wants her to give up some of her paper route. Angie does not want to do this. She likes the money she makes too much.

Matt is a poor loser. He always wants to be the winner. If someone else wins, he gets very angry. When asked what he wants to be when he grows up, Matt says he wants to be his own boss. "The most important thing," he says, "is looking out for number one—me."

Imagine that you have been asked to give a talk to the third grade. What suggestions would you give them about putting God first in their lives?

PRACTICING FAITH

Plan your ideas for a poster to show how you will try to live the first commandment this week. Then share these ideas and create a group poster titled "God Comes First." You might want to display it in your parish church.

Close by sharing a prayer of petition. Each one prays:

† Dear God, help us to put you first in our lives by

_____

_____

_____

Talk with your teacher about ways you and your family might use the "Faith Alive" section. Ask family members to share ideas on ways to honor God in their lives.

REVIEW ■ TEST

Circle the letter beside the correct answer.

1. The first commandment tells us to

   a. keep God first in our lives.

   b. honor our parents.

   c. tell the truth.

2. Those things we make more important than God are

   a. commandments.

   b. false gods.

   c. covenants.

3. God gave the commandments to

   a. Jesus.

   b. Joseph.

   c. Moses.

4. In the desert the devil tempted Jesus to

   a. turn stones into bread.

   b. calm a storm.

   c. rise from the dead.

5. How will you put God first in your life?

   _____

   _____

FAITH ALIVE AT HOME AND IN THE PARISH

In this lesson your fourth grader learned that the first commandment tells us to put God first in our lives. Putting God first in one's life is always a challenge. With many parents holding down two jobs, caring for an aging parent, or facing serious family illness, it is easy to lose focus in life. Yet the most ancient roots of our faith tell us that it is not only a law but very wise to put God first. This helps us to keep things in perspective.

Remember, too, that God is always present to us, reaching out in love to sustain and strengthen us.

God is our creator, our redeemer, and our sustainer. Only God deserves our praise and worship—God alone. Keeping God first is essential in our lives. It is the wisest and happiest way we can live.

Putting God First in Our Family

Make a "God Comes First" poster. Write on the poster things that you and your family do to honor God. Some of these things might be praying, thanking him for some gift, going to Mass, or doing something for people in need. Hang the completed poster in a place where everyone can see it.

11 God's Name Is Holy
The Second Commandment

Lamb of God, you take away the sin of the world. Give us peace.

Our Life

A young boy named Corey was in a very serious accident. He was rushed to the hospital in a coma. The doctors were worried about him because he showed no signs of coming out of the coma. The family took turns staying with Corey and talking quietly to him.

One day after visiting the hospital's chapel, Corey's father went to his son's room. He stood at the foot of the bed and called his son's name in a loud voice, "Corey!" At that moment, Corey's eyes slowly opened. He smiled at his father.

What do you learn from this story?

What does a person's name really stand for?

How do I show respect for a person's name?

Sharing Life

Talk together about the names you have for God.

What are some things you think of when you hear God's name—for example, love?

Why do you think we should show respect for God's name?

Make a list of all the names and descriptions you know for God. Print each one in large block letters. Cut the letters out. Now attach the names and descriptions to a string of crepe paper or yarn and put it across the front of the room.

Each day this week, choose one of the names or descriptions as part of your prayer to God.

This week we will discover more about God's holy name.

We Will Learn

- The Israelites were taught how to keep God's name and places holy.

- Jesus shows us how to respect God's name and holy places.

- We live the second commandment by respecting the name of God, the name of Jesus, and holy places.

Loving God, you call us each by name. We are yours. Why should we treat people's names with respect?

God's Holy Name

The people of Israel believed that respecting a person's name was a way of showing respect for that person. They showed special respect for God's name as given to Moses.

God told Moses, "I am who am . . . you must tell the Israelites: I AM sent me to you . . . . This is my name forever."

Exodus 3:14–15

The words "I am who I am" make up the Hebrew word *Yahweh*. Yahweh was the name the Israelites called God.

The second commandment of God is "You shall not take the name of the LORD, your God, in vain" (Exodus 20:7). The people of Israel had such great respect for God's name that they did not speak his name out loud.

Jesus taught his disciples to pray to God, saying, "Our Father, who art in heaven, hallowed be thy name." The word *hallowed* means holy and worthy of praise. Jesus was telling the disciples that God's name is truly holy. We must use God's name with great respect and praise him.

Respecting Holy Places

Jesus also respected holy places that honored God. One time, Jesus went to the Temple in Jerusalem to pray. Some people were using the Temple as a place to buy and sell things.

Jesus chased them out of the Temple. He said, "It is written:
'My house shall be a house of prayer', but you are making it a den of thieves."

Matthew 21:12–13

We obey the second commandment when we show respect for our parish church and its property. The commandment also reminds us that our conduct in church should always help others to pray and never be a distraction.

We should also show respect for the places of worship used by other Christians, Jews, and people of other religions. We would want them to do the same for us.

FAITH WORD

To **respect** means to show honor to someone or something.

The second commandment reminds us that God's name is holy. God's name and all places that honor God must always be treated with honor and respect. When we do this, we give honor and respect to God. We live the second commandment. We show we are living for God's kingdom, as Jesus taught us.

What did you learn from the story of Jesus in the Temple?

How will you show respect for your parish church?

109

Our Catholic Faith

Choose one of your favorite names for God. Repeat it silently and slowly several times.

Why do you think we should show reverence for the name of Jesus?

The Holy Name of Jesus

We must also show respect for the holy name of Jesus. Saint Paul tells us that God gave Jesus the name that is greater than any other name. And so, everyone must honor the name of Jesus and say "Jesus Christ is Lord."

Based on Philippians 2:9–11

Jesus is the Word of God; Jesus is the Son of God and our Savior. That is why the name of Jesus is very special to everyone in the Christian community. We are to use God's holy name and the name of Jesus Christ with respect and love.

The first Christians had great respect for the name of Jesus. We read in the Bible that one time the apostles Peter and John went to the Temple. At one of the Temple gates, there was a man who could not walk and was begging for money.

Peter said, "I have neither silver nor gold, but what I do have I give you: in the name of Jesus Christ the Nazorean, [rise and] walk."

At once, the man got up and began to walk. He went into the temple with Peter and John to praise and thank God.

Acts of the Apostles 3:6

This event, and others like it, taught the first Christians great respect for Jesus' name.

Keeping God's Name Holy

We must always use God's holy name and the holy name of Jesus Christ with love and great respect.

Sometimes people use God's name or Jesus' name when they are angry. They use God's name to curse, or wish bad things, on someone. To use God's name or Jesus' name in vain is wrong and is a sin.

Sometimes we are asked to swear on God's name that something is true. Swearing is calling on God to be our witness.

Witnesses in court swear, or call on God, to witness that they are telling the truth. Swearing is only for serious occasions such as this. It is a very serious sin to swear on God's name and then to tell lies.

We are disrespectful to God's name and Jesus' name when we use them in vain. We take God's name in vain when we use it for no reason other than to express our anger or to "show off."

God's name is holy. As God's people, we must be holy in all that we do. Saint Peter told the first Christians, "Be holy yourselves in every aspect of your conduct," just as God is holy.

Based on 1 Peter 1:15

How can we show that we respect God and Jesus Christ by what we say and do?

Decide now how you will avoid using God's name or the name of Jesus Christ in vain.

OUR CATHOLIC FAITH

■ Sing "Holy God, We Praise Thy Name" as your opening prayer (page 114).

■ Why do Catholics show respect for holy people and things?

Living the Commandment

God's name and everything that belongs to him are very special. We use all things of God with love and respect. We show how much we love Jesus by the way we say his name. Saint Paul once wrote that in honor of the name of Jesus, all beings should fall on their knees.

Based on Philippians 2:10

We also treat holy people and things with respect because they remind us of God. We are to respect the house of God and be respectful in church. We treat all things in our churches with care and respect.

Ask the Holy Spirit to guide you in keeping the second commandment, in growing as a respectful member of the Church, and in building up God's kingdom. You may also wish to share together this prayer from the Mass of the Holy Name of Jesus.

may we who honor the holy name of Jesus,
enjoy his friendship in this life,
and be filled with eternal joy in his kingdom,
where he lives and reigns with you and the Holy Spirit,
one God, for ever and ever.

Describing God

The Church has always taught that our human words fall short in naming or describing God. God is a mystery. He is not like anyone or anything in the whole universe. He is perfect. God created the universe—no one created God.

In the Bible we find many names and descriptions of God that help us to pray and to know his love for us. God is described as loving, kind, merciful, just, tender, faithful, caring, and much more.

Other descriptions or names of God in the Bible come from nature. God is described as a rock, a mountain, light, a gentle breeze, and so on. God is also called Father, King, and Lord.

Besides masculine descriptions and names, feminine words are also used in the Bible to describe God.

For example, God is compared to a mother. The prophet Isaiah tells us that God says,
"As a mother comforts her son,
so will I comfort you" (Isaiah 66:13).

Perhaps the most important description of God in the Bible is "God is love" (1 John 4:8).

Share with a friend your favorite name or description of God.

Learn by heart **Faith Summary**

- The second commandment is "You shall not take the name of the Lord your God, in vain."

- We live the second commandment by respecting God's name, the name of Jesus, and holy places.

- Cursing is wishing evil on someone. Swearing is calling on God to be our witness that we are telling the truth.

Coming to Faith

How should we live the second commandment? Tell what you would say about Leo and Janine.

Leo says that all his friends swear and curse, using God's name. Leo does not want to be different from the others so he swears too.

Janine is your very good friend. You really like her. But Janine often uses the name of Jesus in a disrespectful way. She says she just does it to be funny.

Practicing Faith

We have many names that describe God. Each one is a word of praise for his goodness and greatness. Think of your favorite name for God. Write it here.

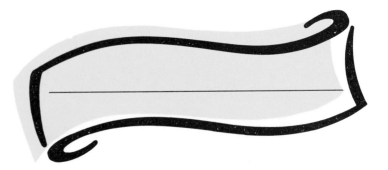

Gather with your friends in a circle. Take turns sharing your favorite names for God. Tell why they are your favorites. Then pray:

† O God, we love your name. (Each one, in turn, softly calls aloud the name of God he or she chose.) We will honor your name always. Amen.

Sing together:

Holy God, we praise thy name;
Lord of all, we bow before thee;
All on earth thy scepter claim.
All in heaven above adore thee;
Infinite, thy vast domain,
Everlasting is thy reign.

Talk with your teacher about ways you and your family might use the "Faith Alive" section. Plan time to work together to make a Jesus banner.

REVIEW · TEST

Circle the letter beside the correct answer.

1. The second commandment tells us to

   a. keep the Sabbath holy.

   b. obey our parents.

   c. use God's name with respect.

2. Showing honor to someone or something is

   a. cursing.

   b. swearing.

   c. respect.

3. Calling on God to be our witness is

   a. cursing.

   b. obeying.

   c. swearing.

4. Wishing bad things to happen to someone is

   a. cursing.

   b. swearing.

   c. lying.

5. How can you show respect for your parish church?

   _____

   _____

FAITH ALIVE AT HOME AND IN THE PARISH

In this chapter your fourth grader learned about obeying the second commandment and about honoring God's name, the holy name of Jesus, and holy places. Showing reverence for God's holy name and the holy name of Jesus is an important commandment of our Catholic faith. Likewise, when we take an oath, we call on God to be our witness. This is a sacred use of God's name and must never be done in vain.

God's Holy Name

Sometimes we forget how much the language we use influences those around us. Decide as a family to use God's holy name only with respect.

A Jesus Banner

Work together to make a banner that bears the holy name of Jesus. Perhaps you can find a place to hang it in your home. It can be a family reminder of the respect due to the name of God's Son.

12 | We Worship God
The Third Commandment

OUR LIFE

It was late Friday afternoon. Rebecca was going home from school with her best friend, Nora. When they got there, Rebecca's mother had already prepared the evening meal and was getting ready to light the special Sabbath candles. Rebecca and her family are Jews and practice the Jewish religion.

Nora said to Rebecca, "I thought that the Jewish Sabbath was on Saturday."

"Our Jewish Sabbath begins on Friday night," said Rebecca. "The rabbi told us that in the Bible people describe each day as beginning the evening before. Our Sabbath day begins at sunset on Friday and ends at sunset on Saturday."

Nora explained, "The Christian Sabbath is on Sunday to remember the day Jesus rose from the dead."

Tell some of the things that you and your family do to make Sunday special.

SHARING LIFE

Do you think it is important to keep Sunday a holy day? Why or why not?

Share together how Christians can grow in keeping our Sabbath holy.

Here is a special invitation to you.

Jesus invites you to a celebration of the Eucharist in which we will worship God, listen to God's word, and receive Jesus in Holy Communion.

Date: this weekend
Time: a Mass of your choice
Place: your parish church
RSVP: (today's date)

Do you know what RSVP means? It means "please respond."

Do you think it is important to answer an invitation with RSVP? Explain.

In the space below, write your response to Jesus' invitation. Tell him when you will meet him at Mass this week. Share the invitation and your response with your family.

Dear Jesus,

_____

_____

_____

_____

_____

_____

_____

_____

This week we will discover ways to follow the third commandment.

We Will Learn

- The Israelites kept the Sabbath holy to obey God's third commandment.

- Christians celebrate their Sabbath on Sunday.

- We live the third commandment by keeping Sunday and other special days holy.

One Sabbath, Jesus went to eat a meal at the home of an important Pharisee. The people who were there watched Jesus closely when a man whose arms and legs were swollen went up to him.

Jesus knew that some of the people did not understand the true meaning of the Sabbath. They thought that resting from work included resting from good works as well. So he asked, "Is it lawful to cure on the sabbath or not?" But they would not say a word.

For rest and shelter in the night, loving God, we thank you. For each new morning with its light, loving God, we thank you.

Why do you think God gave us the commandment to keep a Sabbath day?

The Sabbath in Israel

The third commandment that God gave Moses was "Remember to keep holy the sabbath day" (Exodus 20:8).

The people of Israel celebrated the Sabbath every week, beginning on Friday evening and ending on Saturday evening. They honored and worshiped God, the creator of all things. They rested from their work and went to the synagogue to pray.

Jesus and the Sabbath

As a young boy, Jesus celebrated the Sabbath with his family. He also went with them to the Temple in Jerusalem to worship God on special holy days. Later he taught his disciples the true meaning of the Sabbath.

118

The word **Sabbath** comes from a Jewish word that means "rest."

Then Jesus took the man, healed him, and sent him away. Jesus said to the Pharisees, "Who among you, if your son or ox falls into a cistern, would not immediately pull him out on the sabbath day?"

But they were not able to answer this question either.

Based on Luke 14:1–6

Jesus taught the importance of putting time aside to honor and worship God.

He taught us the importance of the Sabbath. But he also taught us that we must never rest from being his disciples and doing good works. By doing this, we follow his way and keep holy the Sabbath.

How did the people of Israel celebrate the Sabbath?

How will you keep the Lord's day holy this week?

119

OUR CATHOLIC FAITH

God of all, help us come before you with praise and thanksgiving.

Tell some of the ways that you like to keep the Sabbath holy.

The Christian Sabbath

From the beginning of the Church, Christians have celebrated their Sabbath on Sunday. The first Christians remembered that Jesus rose from the dead on Easter Sunday. Sunday became the Lord's special day and our Christian Sabbath.

Today Christians celebrate Sunday by setting aside time to rest, to turn to God, and to worship God as a community. Catholics come together as a parish community to celebrate the Mass. We listen to the word of God and receive Jesus in Holy Communion. We leave Mass ready to serve God by serving others.

The Catholic Church teaches that attending Mass on Sunday or on Saturday evening is a serious obligation. This means that Catholics must take part in the Mass unless there is a very good reason for missing it, such as serious sickness.

We may anticipate, or look ahead, to Sunday Mass by celebrating it on Saturday evening. When it is not possible for us to go to Mass, we should try to read the Scriptures and say our prayers at home.

All of us have a serious responsibility to try our best to take part in the Mass on Saturday evening or Sunday. Resting from unnecessary work is also part of keeping this day holy.

We need to think about doing God's will by loving God and our neighbor better during the coming week. We also think of what it means to live for God's kingdom. In these ways we live the third commandment, "Remember to keep holy the Sabbath day."

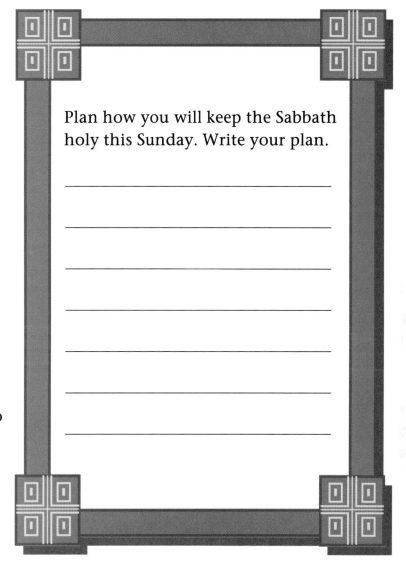

Plan how you will keep the Sabbath holy this Sunday. Write your plan.

_____

_____

_____

_____

_____

_____

Why is Sunday the Christian Sabbath day?

What one thing will you do better this week to keep the Sabbath holy? Be specific.

- Begin by singing together "Holy God, We Praise Thy Name." (See page 114.)

- In what ways can we "rest" on Sunday?

Living the Commandment

The Church also teaches that on Sundays we must try to rest, especially from unnecessary work. We keep the Sabbath holy by taking time to take care of our minds and bodies. We also try to spend fun time with our family and friends.

There are also other days that we try to keep holy. These are called holy days of obligation. These days remind us to celebrate some event in the life of Jesus Christ, the Blessed Virgin Mary, or the other saints.

HOLY DAYS OF OBLIGATION

In the United States, Catholics must go to Mass on these holy days of obligation:

Mary, Mother of God
(January 1)

Ascension
(during the Easter season)

Assumption of Mary
(August 15)

All Saints' Day
(November 1)

Immaculate Conception
(December 8)

Christmas
(December 25)

Time for God

The Church reminds us that it is important to be on time for Mass. When we deliberately choose to arrive late for the celebration of the Eucharist, we show disrespect for the assembly and for God.

It is a good practice to arrive a few minutes early for Mass. It gives us time to pray quietly and think about the tremendous things that are about to happen in the celebration of the Eucharist. It is a good time to kneel and pray to Jesus, who is present in the Blessed Sacrament. The lighted sanctuary lamp reminds us that the Blessed Sacrament is in the tabernacle.

Just as we should arrive early, we must not leave Mass before the celebration is completed. Each part of the Mass is important. Unless we have a good excuse, we should plan on being at the entire celebration so that we may worship God fully with our community.

Learn by heart ## Faith Summary

- The third commandment is "Remember to keep holy the Sabbath day."

- Christians celebrate their Sabbath on Sunday. We remember that Jesus rose from the dead on Easter Sunday.

- Catholics must take part in the Mass on Sunday or on Saturday evening and on all holy days of obligation.

123

COMING TO FAITH

Change each story to show the third commandment being lived.

Kathy goes to Sunday Mass because her mother makes her go. All through Mass, Kathy wishes that she were somewhere else. She never pays attention or joins in the Mass.

George always waits until Sunday to do his homework. He says that he does not have time to go to Mass, because he must spend all day Sunday doing his book reports and other assignments.

Imagine that you have a friend who belongs to another religion, or has no religion at all. Explain to your friend why Catholics celebrate Mass on Sunday. What would you say?

Are you glad we have Sunday as a day to rest and to celebrate our faith? Why or why not?

PRACTICING FAITH

How will you make Sunday a holy day for you?

Finish these sentences by drawing or writing what you will try to do.

I will take time off for fun and recreation by...

I will worship God by...

I will take time to be with my friends and family by...

Talk with your teacher about ways you and your family might use the "Faith Alive" section. Plan a Sunday celebration with your family.

REVIEW ▪ TEST

Circle the letter beside the correct answer.

1. The third commandment is

a. Honor your father and mother.

b. Remember to keep holy the Sabbath day.

c. You shall not steal.

2. Every week the people of Israel celebrated the

a. Passover.

b. Seder.

c. Sabbath.

3. On Sunday or Saturday evening and on holy days of obligation, Catholics are obliged to take part in

a. the Mass.

b. the rosary.

c. Reconciliation.

4. One of the holy days of obligation is

a. Good Friday.

b. Pentecost.

c. Immaculate Conception.

5. How can you prepare for Sunday Mass?

_____

_____

FAITH ALIVE AT HOME AND IN THE PARISH

In this lesson your fourth grader learned the third commandment and why Christians keep Sunday as their Sabbath day. On Sunday we remember and celebrate the resurrection of Jesus, who brought us new life. Each Sunday should be a special time of prayer, rest, and fun. The word *Sabbath* literally means "rest." Keeping the Sabbath holy and as a day of rest is one of the richest aspects of our faith tradition as Catholics. In our busy modern world, we are once again challenged to learn what it means to keep the Sabbath day holy.

Help your fourth grader develop the habit of participating in the celebration of Mass each Sunday or Saturday evening.

Celebrating a Family Sabbath

Each Sunday should be a special time of rest and prayer. This Sunday, have a special celebration with your family. Attend Mass together. Share a special meal. Do something fun together as a family that allows you to enjoy one another's company.

†A Sabbath Prayer

Our loving God, You have given us our Sabbath day for worship and rest. Recreate a happy heart in us, O God, as we come together in your name. Amen.

13 | Celebrating Advent

God, we are
your servants.
May we live
your loving
will always.

OUR LIFE

The town of Nazareth was coming awake after a long, peaceful night. Women began to fill their jars with water from the village well. One of them was Mary.

Mary had a secret that she kept inside her heart. The angel Gabriel had come to her from God and had asked her to be the mother of God's Son.

Mary remembered the angel's words: "You will bear . . . a son . . .. He will . . . be called Son of the Most High."

Quietly, Mary repeated the answer she had given to the angel: "I am the handmaid of the Lord. May it be done to me according to your word."

Mary had to get ready. She decided to visit her cousin Elizabeth. The angel had told Mary that Elizabeth was also about to have a baby. Mary made the long, difficult journey to visit and help her cousin, who was much older than Mary.

Mary stayed for about three months, until Elizabeth's son, John, was born. Then Mary went back home to wait for her own baby to be born.
Based on Luke 1:26–39, 56

What do you think Mary did during those months of waiting for Jesus to be born?

Have you ever waited for a younger sister or brother or cousin to be born? What did your family do to get ready?

SHARING LIFE

How do you feel as you wait to celebrate Jesus' birth on Christmas?

What are some of the best ways to get ready for Christmas?

126

ADVENT PROJECT

Project (explain it)

_____

_____

What needs to be done:

_____

_____

Who does what:

_____

_____

When we will do it:

_____

_____

How kind it was of Mary to go and help her cousin Elizabeth! Mary's example can help us think of kind acts to do during Advent. Who needs our help in our parish or school or neighborhood? What can we do together to follow Mary's example?

List all the ideas presented so that everyone can see them. Then choose one project on which your group can work together during Advent.

When the project has been chosen, plan how you will go about it.

We Will Learn

- Mary prepared for the birth of Jesus.

- Mary's example can help us to prepare for the birth of Jesus at Christmas.

- We pray the Angelus and the Magnificat.

OUR CATHOLIC FAITH

A Time to Prepare

Advent is the season in which we prepare for the Lord's coming as Mary did. We prepare for the celebration of Jesus' birth at Christmas. We also remember with Mary that Jesus will come again at the end of time.

To get ready for the coming of Jesus, here are some things you might do:

- Help out at home. For example, take care of a younger child, set the table, wash the dishes, take out the garbage.

- Be extra kind to someone. For example, do something special for a tired parent, cheer up a lonely person, include someone in your group who is usually left out.

We remember that Mary prepared for Jesus' birth. We can ask Mary to help us to prepare for Christmas by remembering other people's needs, as she did.

Advent Prayers

After Elizabeth greeted Mary, Mary said a beautiful prayer of praise to God. We call it the Magnificat. Part of this prayer can be found on this page. Maybe you would like to pray it during Advent.

During Advent, we can also pray the Angelus. *Angelus* is a Latin word that means "angel." The Angelus prayer helps us to remember the time when the angel came to Mary. We remember that Mary said yes and became the mother of God's own Son.

Try to learn the Angelus by heart. You will find it on text page 130.

The Magnificat

My soul proclaims the
   greatness of the Lord;
   my spirit rejoices in
   God my savior.
For he has looked upon his
   handmaid's lowliness;
   behold, from now on will all
   ages call me blessed.
The Mighty One has done great
   things for me,
   and holy is his name.
His mercy is from age to age
   to those who fear him.
Luke 1:46–50

COMING TO FAITH

Spend this Advent with Mary. Try to look at your world as she would. What might Mary do if she were living now in your family or in your neighborhood?

What will you do to prepare with Mary to celebrate Jesus' coming? Write it here.

_____

_____

Practicing Faith

We Honor Mary
An Advent Prayer Service

Opening Hymn: Hail Mary

Leader: We come together to give honor to Mary, the mother of Jesus and our mother, too. We remember how Mary said yes and became the mother of God's Son. We ask Mary to help us to be like her as we prepare to celebrate Christmas. Let us pray the Angelus together.

Side 1: The angel of the Lord declared to Mary,

Side 2: and she conceived by the Holy Spirit.

All: Hail Mary. . . .(Pray the Hail Mary together.)

Side 1: Behold the handmaid of the Lord,

Side 2: be it done to me according to your word.

All: Hail Mary. . . .

Side 1: And the Word was made flesh

Side 2: and dwelled among us.

All: Hail Mary. . . .

Side 1: Pray for us, O Holy Mother of God,

Side 2: that we may be made worthy of the promises of Christ.

Leader: Let us pray.

All: Pour forth, we beseech you, O Lord, your grace into our hearts that we to whom the incarnation of Christ your Son was made known by the message of an angel may, by his passion and death, be brought to the glory of his resurrection, through the same Christ our Lord. Amen.

Closing Hymn

Sing to the tune of "Clementine."

Mother Mary, Blessed Mother,
We all pray to you each day.
Please help us to get ready
for your Son on Christmas day.

REVIEW ▪ TEST

Write one thing you know about each one.

1. Mary _____

_____

2. Elizabeth _____

_____

3. Gabriel _____

_____

4. What prayers to Mary can you pray during Advent?
When will you do this?

_____

_____

FAITH ALIVE AT HOME AND IN THE PARISH

In this chapter Advent was presented as a time to prepare for Christmas by remembering the needs of others. The word *Advent* comes from the Latin verb *advenire*, which means "to come." During Advent we remember and prepare to celebrate the coming of Jesus Christ, both at Christmas and at the end of time.

The Advent gospel readings proclaim the final coming of Jesus Christ in glory at the end of time. In the Christian life, the best way to prepare for the end of time is by living our faith now as disciples of Jesus. This is why we listen to the message of John the Baptist to prepare the way of the Lord by changing our lives and hearts.

Learn by heart **Faith Summary**

- Mary prepared for Jesus by helping others.

- We prepare for Christmas by remembering the needs of others.

Jesus, Mary, and Joseph, bless us and bless our families.

Our Life

Jesus, Mary, and Joseph lived in Nazareth. The town was filled with small houses built close to one another. Most of the houses had flat roofs, where the people would sit and talk in the evening.

We can imagine what life must have been like for the Holy Family.

Every day Mary baked bread for her family. She served fruits and vegetables and sometimes fish or meat for dinner. Jesus, Mary, and Joseph prayed before and after each meal.

Joseph was a carpenter and taught Jesus how to use carpenter's tools. Mary and Joseph taught Jesus how to love, how to pray, and how to live according to God's law.

Just like families today, there were many times when Jesus, Mary, and Joseph laughed together. Sometimes they must have been sad. They must have talked about what the future might hold for Jesus.

Do you think Jesus, Mary, and Joseph did any of the things you do every day? Which ones?

Sharing Life

Imagine what it might be like if you could go back in time to visit the home of Jesus, Mary, and Joseph. Talk with your friends about what you would do. What might you say? Is there anything you would ask them to help you with?

Now picture some of the events of this wonderful Christmas season. Choose a gospel scene that you especially like and make a Christmas tree ornament showing this scene. Use the space below to design your ornament. Trace it and cut it out. Be sure to leave room at the top so that you can hang it on the tree.

Share your ornament with the group. Tell why you chose the scene you did.

We Will Learn

- We celebrate some important feasts during the Christmas season.

- We celebrate the feast of the Holy Innocents on December 28.

- We also celebrate feasts of the Holy Family and of Mary.

133

OUR CATHOLIC FAITH

We Celebrate Christmas

The Christmas season is a special time to remember and pray to the Holy Family. We celebrate the birth of Jesus, our Savior, in Bethlehem. We also celebrate other important feasts during the season of Christmas.

Holy Innocents

On December 28, we celebrate the feast of the Holy Innocents. The Holy Innocents were children whom King Herod ordered to be killed. Their story is told in the Gospel of Matthew.

When Jesus was born in Bethlehem, some visitors from the east came to King Herod in Jerusalem. They told Herod that a special star had guided them and that they had come to worship a baby born to be a king.

Herod was afraid of losing his throne to the newborn king. So he told the visitors to go to Bethlehem. He pretended that he wanted to know where the child was, so that he could worship him, too.

The visitors found Jesus with Mary and Joseph. But they were warned by God in a dream not to tell King Herod. Joseph also had a dream. Joseph was told in the dream to take Mary and Jesus to Egypt for safety.

When King Herod realized that the visitors had tricked him and had gone home, he ordered his soldiers to go to Bethlehem and kill all boys who were two years old and younger.

Based on Matthew 2:1–16

Holy Family

On the Sunday following Christmas, we celebrate the feast of the Holy Family. We remember that Jesus, Mary, and Joseph lived together as a family in Nazareth.

There they worked, prayed, and played together. On the feast of the Holy Family, we ask Jesus, Mary, and Joseph to bless our families and to help us to live for the kingdom of God.

Mary, Mother of God

During the Christmas season, we celebrate a special feast to honor Mary as the Mother of God. On January 1, we remember that eight days after Jesus was born, Mary and Joseph took him to the Temple.

There the baby was named Jesus, the name the angel had given to Mary. The name Jesus means "God saves." We pray to Mary and remember that the Mother of God is our mother, too.

Epiphany
On the Sunday between January 2 and January 8, we celebrate the feast of the Epiphany. Epiphany is a word meaning "manifestation" or "showing forth." On this day we celebrate the showing forth of Jesus as the Light of the World. We hear the story of the wise men who came from a faraway land to worship Jesus, the newborn king.

COMING TO FAITH

Sometimes we think of Christmas as just December 25. But in the Church, the season of Christmas extends from Christmas Day to the feast of the Baptism of the Lord, the Sunday after Epiphany.

Form three groups. Each group will choose a way to share one of the feasts of the Christmas season. You can use music, drama, art, and of course, Scripture.

You might like to present your program to another group in your parish.

PRACTICING FAITH

A Christmas Prayer Service

Make a family Christmas ornament. Cut a decorative shape out of paper. Write on this shape the names of the people who make up your family. Then decorate your special ornament.

Opening Hymn

O come, all ye faithful, joyful and triumphant,
O come ye, O come ye to Bethlehem;
Come and behold him, born the King of angels;
O come, let us adore him,
O come, let us adore him,
O come, let us adore him,
Christ the Lord!

Leader: On the feast of the Holy Family, we come together to honor Jesus, Mary, and Joseph. We ask them to bless our families with love, joy, and peace.

Prayer Action

Each one reads the names on his or her ornaments. Then each one places the ornaments on a Christmas tree or display stand.

Leader: Let us pray for our families.

All: Holy Family, help us to live as you did. Help us to love and honor one another in our families. Mary and Joseph, help us to live together in peace and love and to follow the way of Jesus, our Savior. Amen.

Closing Hymn

O little town of Bethlehem,
How still we see thee lie!
Above thy deep and dreamless sleep
The silent stars go by;
Yet in thy dark streets shineth
The everlasting Light:
The hopes and fears of all the years
Are met in thee tonight.

Talk with your teacher about ways you and your family might use the "Faith Alive" section. Plan special ways to remember the feasts during the Christmas season.

REVIEW ▪ TEST

Tell what we celebrate on each of these Christmas feasts.

1. Holy Innocents _____

_____

2. Holy Family _____

_____

3. Mary, Mother of God _____

_____

4. Epiphany _____

_____

5. What do these words from "O Little Town of Bethlehem" mean to you?
"Yet in thy dark streets shineth/the everlasting Light"

_____

_____

FAITH ALIVE AT HOME AND IN THE PARISH

In this chapter your fourth grader learned about some feasts in the liturgical season of Christmas. The Christmas season begins with the vigil Mass on Christmas Eve and ends with the feast of the Baptism of the Lord. During Christmas we celebrate the manifestations of Jesus Christ in our lives and in human history. Jesus is revealed to shepherds, to poor and simple people, and to strangers from the east.

On the great feast of Epiphany, we hear the story of the wise men's search for the newborn King of the Jews. This feast celebrates the epiphany, or manifestation, of God to all people. On the feast of the Baptism of the Lord,

Jesus is revealed as God's own Son. Each of these feasts deepens our appreciation of God's greatest gift to us—Jesus.

Learn by heart **Faith Summary**

- The Christmas season includes the feasts of the Holy Innocents, Holy Family, Mary, Mother of God, and Epiphany.

- The name Jesus means "God saves."

- The Holy Family is Jesus, Mary, and Joseph.

137

15 Loving Our Parents
The Fourth Commandment

Jesus, Mary, and Joseph, bless our family now and always. Amen.

OUR LIFE

When Jesus was twelve years old, he went to Jerusalem with Mary and Joseph along with other family members and friends for the great Passover festival. After Passover, Mary and Joseph started home without Jesus. They thought he was returning with friends. When they discovered that he was not with them, Mary and Joseph rushed back to Jerusalem. After three days, they found Jesus in the Temple asking the teachers questions.

Mary was upset. She said, "Son, why have you done this to us? Your father and I have been looking for you with great anxiety."

Jesus said, "Why were you looking for me? Did you not know that I must be in my Father's house?"

Then Jesus went home with Mary and Joseph and was obedient to them.
Based on Luke 2:41–51

How do you think Mary and Joseph felt while they were looking for Jesus?

How do you show obedience to your parents or guardians?

SHARING LIFE

Work in two groups to develop your responses to these questions. Then share your ideas with everyone.

Group 1: Why should children obey the adults in their families?

Group 2: Why should we show respect to older people?

Now think about ways you can show respect for others. Complete this chart. Then share your responses with the whole group.

Person	Ways I Can Show Respect
a grandparent	
the pope	
the president of our country	
a police officer	
an elderly neighbor	
my teachers	

You might want to look back at your chart as we learn more about the fourth commandment this week.

We Will Learn

- The Israelites obeyed God's commandment to respect their parents.
- Jesus shows us how to love and honor our parents.
- We can love and honor our parents in many ways.

■ Mary, mother of Jesus, pray for us.

■ How do you show respect for your parents?

Respect for Parents

God did not make people to be alone. When God created people, he created a man and a woman. God told the man and the woman to have many children and to fill the earth.

Based on Genesis 1:27–28

God created us to live as a family. In every family, some members care for those not yet ready or not able to care for themselves.

God wants us to honor and obey those who care for us and who are responsible for us. In the fourth commandment, God tells us, "Honor your father and your mother" (Exodus 20:12).

The people of Israel obeyed this commandment from God and had a special respect for parents. They also respected anyone in positions of authority or leadership.

Older people were given special honor, too. One of the reasons is that they had learned much wisdom in their lives, wisdom that they would share with all the people.

This made older people treasured members of the community and deserving of the respect that God had commanded of the people. God told the people of Israel, "show respect for the old" (Leviticus 19:32).

Jesus and His Parents

Jesus also showed us how to love and honor those who care for us.

The Holy Family of Mary, Joseph, and Jesus worked and played, prayed and worshiped together. Mary, Jesus' mother, and Joseph, his foster father, taught him the Jewish prayers and God's commandments. They taught Jesus how to love and to care for others, especially the poor and people in need.

One time, when Jesus was grown up, he went to a wedding at Cana in Galilee. His mother Mary was there, too. During the wedding feast, the wine ran out. Mary told Jesus that there was no wine. At first, Jesus said, "My hour has not yet come." But Mary told the servants, "Do whatever he tells you."

Jesus meant that he did not feel ready to start his great public mission for God's kingdom. However, he told the waiters at the feast to fill six big jars with water. When the waiters tasted it, they found that the water had become the best wine of all.

Based on John 2:1–10

FAITH WORD

To **honor** means to show respect and reverence for another.

Jesus was the Son of God and Mary's Son, too. He worked the miracle of changing water into wine by his divine power. But he was also showing a deep respect and love for his mother. She had asked him to help care for the people at the feast. As we try to obey the fourth commandment, how wonderful it is to have Jesus' example.

Jesus wants us to honor our parents and those who care for us. We should help them in any way we can. When our parents get older, we must return to them the love and care they gave to us as we were growing up. We must support and care for them.

Jesus also wants us to show respect for older people and for those in positions of authority or leadership. When we do this, we show that we are living for the kingdom, or reign, of God.

- Explain what the fourth commandment requires of us.
- How will you honor and obey your parents better this week?

OUR CATHOLIC FAITH

- Jesus, Mary, Joseph, bless and protect my family.

- When do you find it difficult to obey the fourth commandment?

The Fourth Commandment

Jesus showed us how to follow the fourth commandment. For us, as for Jesus, to obey the fourth commandment means to love and honor our parents or guardians and all who care for us.

Our parents or guardians are our first and most important teachers. They teach us how to love God, others, and ourselves. When we honor and obey those who care for us, we are doing God's loving will for us. Doing God's will always makes us free and brings us true happiness.

Families are made up of people who belong to and care for one another. God wants all families to be happy, but some are not. Parents can have problems that lead them to live apart. When this happens, it might seem to their children that one or the other of their parents does not love them. This is not true.

If you feel this way, speak to your parents about it. You can also talk to a priest, your teachers, or another adult. Jesus does not want you to keep your hurts inside you.

We keep the fourth commandment by obeying all those who take care of us in any way. We respect our teachers and those who lead us. We respect our state and country by trying to be good citizens.

After listening to Jesus' words, the Church reminds us that as good citizens we should take seriously our obligation to vote, pay taxes, and serve our country. But we should also keep God first in our lives—no matter what.

In all these ways Catholics obey the fourth commandment. When we do this, we grow strong as members of the Church and live for God's kingdom as disciples of Jesus Christ.

Write a prayer asking God to bless your family.

† _____

_____

_____

_____

A good citizen is someone who obeys the just laws of the country.

One time, some people asked Jesus whether they should obey the laws of God or the laws of the Roman emperor. They asked him whether or not they should pay taxes to Caesar.

Jesus said, "Repay to Caesar what belongs to Caesar and to God what belongs to God."
Based on Matthew 22:17, 21

Explain why parents or guardians are our most important teachers.

This week how will you try to honor your parents better? your teachers? your country?

OUR CATHOLIC FAITH

- Silently pray the prayer you wrote for your family. (See page 143.)

- How do you think your family can grow as a community of love?

Living the Commandment

Jesus never promised us that it would be easy to live the fourth commandment. It is not always easy to love and honor those who care for us.

There may be times when we do not want to do what our parents, guardians, or teachers ask us to do. Sometimes parents may be tired and cranky, too. They can lose their patience with their children.

In families, children and adults must try to help one another. Each day we should try to find a quiet moment to hug our parents and tell them how much we love them. We need to tell them of our fears, our worries, as well as the good things that happen to us. This is how we build a community of love in our family and live the fourth commandment.

There may even be times when we should not do what we are asked to do. We need to ask an adult whom we trust to help us when this happens.

In their message to families called "Follow the Way of Love," the American Catholic bishops give families suggestions on ways to build a community of love. They urge us to take time together by sharing family meals. They encourage us to pray and worship together, especially at the Sunday Eucharist and in family prayers such as the rosary. Whatever families can share together can help them to grow in obeying the fourth commandment.

The Presentation of the Lord

The Gospel of Saint Luke tells a wonderful story about the Holy Family. Soon after Jesus was born, Joseph and Mary took him to the Temple in the city of Jerusalem. They did this to follow the Jewish law that the firstborn male child was to be presented, or dedicated, to God.

Each year on February 2, Catholics celebrate the feast of the Presentation of the Lord. On this day we remember the presentation of Jesus in the Temple. We hear the words of Luke's Gospel reminding us that Jesus is the Light of the World. For that reason, this is also the day that the Church chooses to bless candles that will be used for worship all during the year.

The Blessing of Candles

As the ceremony of blessing candles begins, people may gather outside the parish church with unlighted candles. While the candles are being lighted, the people sing a hymn in praise of Christ our Light. Then the priest blesses the candles and asks God to make them holy. He prays that we who carry them to praise God will "walk in the path of goodness and come to the light that shines for ever."

The next time you see lighted candles in church, remember the story of the Holy Family and the feast of the Presentation of the Lord. Pray that you, too, will walk in the path of goodness.

Learn by heart **Faith Summary**

- The fourth commandment is "Honor your father and your mother."

- Jesus showed us how to keep the fourth commandment.

- The fourth commandment teaches us to honor and obey all who take care of us.

COMING TO FAITH

As friends, share together what obeying the fourth commandment means to you.

Tell what you would say to each person in these stories.

John's father has a very bad temper. Sometimes when he is angry, he hits John and his sister. John has just studied the fourth commandment. He wonders whether he can honor his father. He is confused about what to do.

Clara's grandmother has come to live with her family. She is old and does not like noise. Clara's mother has asked her not to play her stereo loudly. Clara is upset because she has to act in a special way now that her grandmother lives with her family.

PRACTICING FAITH

What do you think are important ingredients for a good family life?

Share your ideas with your group and make up a Family Life "recipe." For example, you might want to include ingredients like pounds of respect, cups of love, and tablespoons of honesty. What else needs to be mixed in?

Family Life Recipe

Talk with your teacher about ways you and your family might use the "Faith Alive" section. You might want to work with your family to care for the elderly. Then pray a favorite prayer with your teacher and friends.

146

REVIEW · TEST

Circle the letter beside the correct answer.

1. The fourth commandment is

    a. You shall not kill.

    b. Keep holy the Sabbath day.

    c. Honor your father and mother.

2. Whom did the Israelites honor because of their wisdom?

    a. their enemies

    b. their neighbors

    c. their elders

3. Jesus, Mary, and Joseph are the

    a. Blessed Trinity.

    b. Holy Family.

    c. writers of the gospels.

4. A good citizen must obey the laws of the country that are

    a. just and unjust.

    b. just.

    c. unjust.

5. How can we honor and respect elderly members of our family?

_____

_____

FAITH ALIVE AT HOME AND IN THE PARISH

In this chapter your fourth grader learned that the fourth commandment requires us to love and honor parents, guardians, and all who care for us.

As a parent or guardian you have the responsibility to create a family atmosphere of shared love, honor, and respect that encourages your child to love, obey, and honor you. This can be a great challenge, especially when so many parents are so busy working hard to provide for the basic needs of their families. Remember, too, to pray often that you may follow the example of the Holy Family—Jesus, Mary, and Joseph—and grow as a loving family community.

The Fourth Commandment

The fourth commandment includes respecting and caring for the elderly, first in our own families and then for the elderly in our community. Decide as a family what you can do for those who are "shut-ins" or in nursing homes. You might plan a visit and bring flowers or cards to these people. Your child might make a placemat with a cheerful message. Ask elderly family members to share some of their experiences and stories of the past. They can have great wisdom and faith to share with you and your children.

16 | Living for Life
The Fifth Commandment

Our Life

Look at the pictures. Write "Respecting Life" only in the boxes that show life being respected. Tell why you think this is so. Tell why life is *not* being respected in the other pictures.

What does it mean to respect life?

How do you show respect for all life, including your own?

Sharing Life

Gather in a circle. Take turns responding to each question.

What things help us to be "for life"? What things work "against life"?

Tell some of the best ways to care for your own life.

Why do you think we should care about the lives of others?

Do a magazine search. Work with a partner to select one picture that illustrates respect for life. When everyone is ready, take turns showing the selected picture and explaining why you chose it.

Combine all the pictures on a large posterboard to create a collage or "mosaic" for life. Select a title for your collage and display it in your school. It will help to make what you are going to learn this week about the fifth commandment mean more to you.

We Will Learn

- The Israelites lived the fifth commandment by respecting all life as God's creation.

- Jesus shows us how to choose life.

- We obey the fifth commandment when we care for all life, especially human life.

▪ O God, we are made in your image. Help us always to see your image in ourselves and others.

▪ Why do you think human life is so sacred?

Respecting All Life

From the Bible we know that God made all things good. Of all the living things that God the Father made, people are the most special. That is because human beings are made in the image and likeness of God (See Genesis 1:27). This means that people can think, choose, and love as God does.

Human beings are the only creatures on earth made in God's own image and likeness. Only human beings have God's own life in them.

God's word in the Bible teaches us that every person must be treated with respect. All people have an equal right to life, to freedom, and to be treated with justice. This is why God gave us the fifth commandment, "You shall not kill" (Exodus 20:13).

The fifth commandment teaches us that human life is sacred. We are to respect our lives and the lives of others. We must not kill or hurt ourselves or others.

We must not hurt our own bodies by taking drugs or by using alcohol to excess. We must care for our bodies by getting the right amount of rest, food, and exercise.

We also live the fifth commandment in other ways. We respect others by not fighting with them. We speak up for the right to life of babies waiting to be born. We pray and work for world peace and the end of all war.

The fifth commandment is very clear. We must not deliberately kill or harm anyone. However, as Catholics we know that we do not live in a perfect world. Because of original sin, people throughout history have chosen to sin against this commandment. Our world has witnessed many wars and violent acts against people. What are we as Catholics to do?

The Church teaches us that we also have a responsibility to defend ourselves against evil and protect our lives. In obeying the fifth commandment, we do not look for fights nor are we happy when nations are at war. But when people are unjustly attacked or in danger, this commandment teaches that they should protect themselves.

We must also respect and take care of the world around us. This means that we should not destroy the beauty of any of God's creation. We must not mistreat animals or kill them needlessly. By respecting all of life, especially human life, we obey the fifth commandment and live for God's kingdom of justice and peace.

in YoUr ImagE

Explain what the fifth commandment teaches us about respect for life.

What are some ways that you can keep the fifth commandment? Will you try to do them today?

151

■ Jesus, you came to bring us life, life in all its fullness.

■ What are some of the ways that you show respect for life?

The Fifth Commandment

Jesus showed us how to live the fifth commandment. Jesus treated everyone the way he wants us to treat them—with kindness and patience. Jesus helped the poor and those who were suffering in any way. If people were being kept out by others, Jesus brought them into his community. He fought against all prejudice and discrimination.

Jesus told his followers, "I came so that they might have life and have it more abundantly" (John 10:10). Jesus is our lifegiver. He shows us all how to choose life.

The Church teaches that to choose life we must do much more than avoid committing murder and violent crime. Because we believe that all human life is sacred, we care about all people, especially those who are helpless.

Our Catholic faith reminds us of our special responsibility to care about and protect unborn babies, who cannot protect themselves. We care about the poor, those with special needs, and the elderly. We must respect, care for, and protect all human life. When we care for the needs of all people, we are helping to build a community of peace and justice in our world.

Living the fifth commandment is not always easy. Sometimes we have to make hard choices. For example, when people think that suicide, or taking one's own life, is the easy way out of trouble, they are very wrong. Suicide never solves anything and is a serious offense against God. God gives us the gift of life and the responsibility to care for it. We cannot destroy it for any reason.

Sometimes people let anger and hatred grow in their lives. Jesus says that his disciples try to have God's peace in their hearts. We must never try to get even with those who may have cheated or insulted us. Those who show understanding and forgiveness are the ones who are really strong, brave, and in control.

Remember the words of Jesus who said, "Love your enemies and do good to them" (Luke 6:35).

We choose life and live the fifth commandment when we care about all people and the world around us. If love is in everyone's heart, there is no room for the hate that brings about war.

FAITH WORD

Sacred means belonging to God. Human life is sacred because it belongs to God.

We can work for peace by not being angry with or jealous of others. By keeping the fifth commandment, we do God's will and work for the kingdom of God.

- How did Jesus want his disciples to choose life?

- What will you do today to show that you respect and choose life?

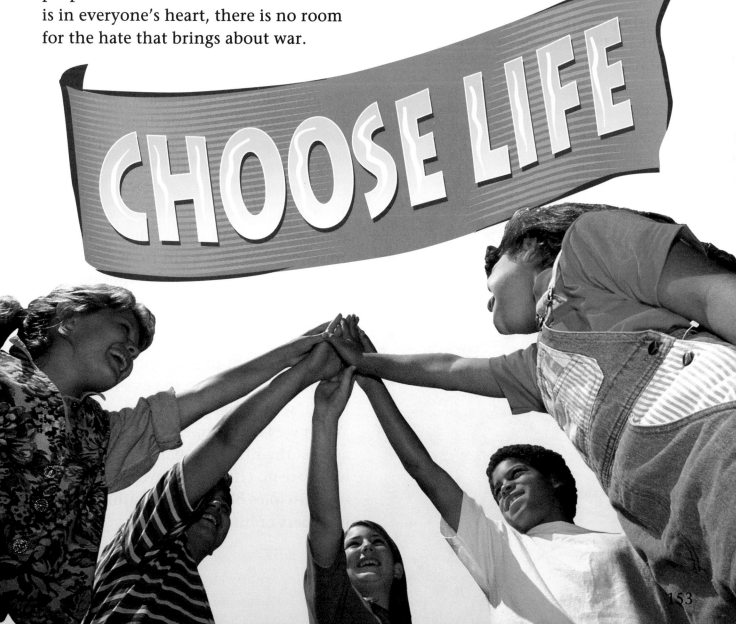

CHOOSE LIFE

153

OUR CATHOLIC FAITH

- Holy Spirit, guide us in choosing to respect all life. Help us to cherish it.

- Explain why each person's life is so important to God.

Living the Commandment

Our bishops write to us as our pastors, or leaders. Their statements are often called pastoral letters.

The bishops in the United States have written a pastoral letter that teaches us how to work for peace and to keep the fifth commandment. It is called "The Challenge of Peace: God's Promise and Our Response."

Cardinal Bernardin, the former archbishop of Chicago, once said that all of life is like a "seamless garment" —a garment, or piece of clothing, made out of one piece of cloth. This means that all living things are united. The way we treat people and every other living thing shows how we feel about life itself.

We also know that there are people who cannot take care of themselves because of sickness or age. Sometimes they have handicaps that cause them great sufferings. The Church teaches us that the lives of these people are as important as those of others. Their presence with us is a gift from God. We have no right to decide whether they live or die. This is for God to decide.

Catholics must respect and work for everyone's right to life—including the unborn, the sick, and the elderly. We have a serious obligation to do so. When we fail to respect life, we sin against the fifth commandment. But when we do choose life, we are being true disciples of Jesus and faithful members of his Church.

Caring for Life

Did you know that the Catholic Church runs many hospitals and other places that care for the sick and the aged? The Church has always carried on Jesus' ministry of promoting life and helping people in pain.

Many religious communities are involved in this kind of healing ministry. For example, the Sisters of Mercy and the Sisters of Charity have built and run many large hospitals in the United States. The Alexian Brothers have a similar ministry.

Through an organization called Catholic Charities, the dioceses of the United States support homes for the elderly and disabled. In our own time, many men, women, and children are suffering from AIDS. The Church is deeply concerned for them and shows Jesus' love by providing places for them to live and to receive treatment, as well as spiritual care and love.

Catholic hospitals and health care facilities are places of love and life. They are always looking for members of the Church to volunteer time in support of their ministry and the people for whom they care. Perhaps one day you can join in their wonderful ministry, too.

Pray together:
† O God, be with all those who are sick or elderly. Comfort them with your great love. Amen.

Learn by heart **Faith Summary**

- The fifth commandment is "You shall not kill." It teaches us that all human life is sacred.

- All people have an equal right to life and to be treated with justice.

- We choose life when we care for all people and the world around us.

COMING TO FAITH

Knowing the fifth commandment, what would you say about these stories?

Kenny likes playing computer games that have a lot of guns and violence. He says it does not hurt anyone.

Lisa says she doesn't see anything wrong with trying drugs just once.

Mark's father told him, "Don't talk to the new neighbors. They are not like us. They belong to a different race."

A chemical company is dumping toxic materials in a river. It's less expensive than handling them according to the law.

PRACTICING FAITH

Work together to write a song about respect for life. Choose an important "life" topic. Pick a tune you know and write your own words to it. You might share the song with your parish.

Then pray together in a life chain. Join hands and silently pray.

† Loving God, life is a beautiful gift. Help us to respect life in ourselves and in others.

End with your group song.

Talk with your teacher about ways you and your family might use the "Faith Alive" section. Spend some time talking with your family about life issues that concern all of you. Pray the Celebrating Family Life prayer with your teacher and friends.

REVIEW ▪ TEST

Circle the letter beside the correct answer.

1. The fifth commandment is

   a. You shall not kill.

   b. You shall not steal.

   c. You shall not swear.

2. The bishops often teach us by writing

   a. gospels.

   b. pastoral letters.

   c. scriptures.

3. When we care for all God's creatures, we choose

   a. safety.

   b. prejudice.

   c. life.

4. Because it belongs to God, human life is

   a. fair.

   b. violent.

   c. sacred.

5. What will you do to care for your own life?

_____

_____

FAITH ALIVE AT HOME AND IN THE PARISH

In this chapter your fourth grader learned that obeying the fifth commandment means choosing life for oneself and others. All of life is like a "seamless garment" made out of only one piece of cloth. This means that if we treat any living thing badly, we hurt all living things. We must respect and work for everyone's right to life. This is how we build up the reign of God as Jesus' disciples. Have a family discussion about the ways we can end any violence around us. Talk about ways that promote a loving respect for life.

Celebrating Family Life

This week we celebrate life, especially human life. Have an "all-together birthday" party. Celebrate everyone's birth. Take time to have each member of the family tell why he or she is glad each person in the family was born. Finish by praying:

✝ God, you have blessed each member of our family with the gift of life. We thank you for this gift and ask you to help us to treat one another with love and respect always. Amen.

17 Faithful in Love
The Sixth and Ninth Commandments

OUR LIFE

Karen had been sick for a long time but now her cancer was in remission. She was thinner and she had lost all her hair in chemotherapy. Karen was nervous about going back to school. How would her classmates react to her?

This is what happened:

- Some said, "Where is your hair? You look funny."

- Some were happy Karen was getting better, but they were uncomfortable and kept away from her.

- Some said, "You are really brave, Karen, and we love you." They made Karen part of everything they did.

Which ones were real friends to Karen?

What does it mean to be a faithful friend?

How do you show that you are one?

SHARING LIFE

Discuss these questions together.

Suppose this group had a friend like Karen. How would we act?

Is it always easy to be a faithful friend?

Do you think that Jesus wants us to be faithful friends? Why?

Friends are flowers in the garden of life.

What do you think this means? Can you come up with another phrase with the same message?

Trace this flowering vine. On the leaves or flowers, write ways you can help a friendship to grow and blossom. Then color the leaves and flowers and cut out the vine. When everyone has finished, connect all the vines.

This week look at the friendship vine often. Ask Jesus to help you to be a faithful friend to him and others.

We Will Learn

- The sixth and ninth commandments help husbands and wives to be faithful to each other.

- Each of us should be faithful in our love of God, family, ourselves, and others.

- We must always choose to love faithfully.

159

▪ Jesus, our Brother and Friend, teach us to be like you—faithful, loyal, and true.

▪ In what ways do you show that you are loyal to your family and friends?

Being Faithful in Marriage

The love that a man and a woman share in marriage is very special. God made mothers and fathers to be equal partners. Married people share their joys and sorrows, their good days and bad days. God asks each woman and man who marry to be loyal and faithful to each other.

The differences between being a man and a woman are gifts from God. These gifts, our sexuality, are an expression of God's great love for us. Sexuality is very sacred and should be used responsibly. In the commandments, God reminds men and women that sexual love should be kept for marriage.

The sixth commandment says, "You shall not commit adultery" (Exodus 20:14). *Adultery* means being unfaithful to one's wife or husband. The ninth commandment says, "You shall not covet your neighbor's wife" (Exodus 20:17). *Covet* means want.

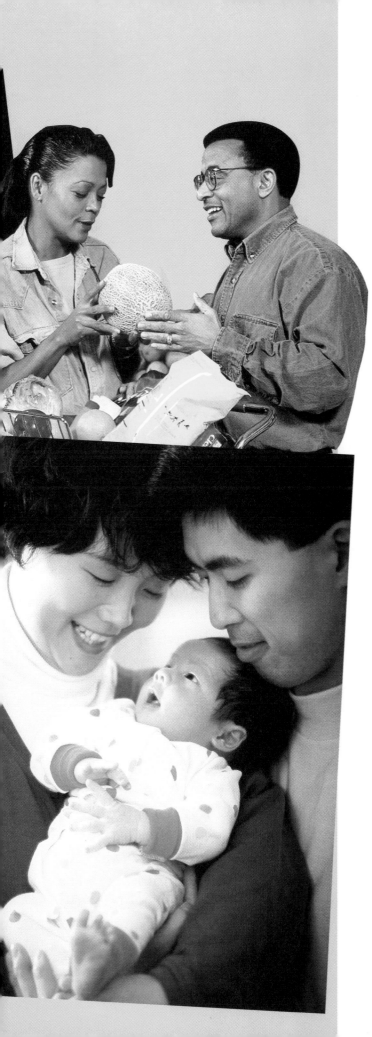

To be **faithful** means to be loyal and true to someone.

The sixth and ninth commandments remind a married couple that no matter how difficult it is, a husband and wife must be faithful to their marriage vows as long as they live. Jesus tells us, "'God made them male and female. For this reason a man shall leave his father and mother [and be joined to his wife], and the two shall become one . . . .' Therefore, what God has joined together, no human being must separate."
Mark 10:6–9

The sixth and ninth commandments also help a husband and wife to create a loving, caring community for their family. The Catholic Church teaches that married couples are to form a community of life and love together.

Families are the heart of God's wonderful world. It is in the family that we are first loved. Through family life, children learn how to do God's will to love him, themselves, and others. Family members work together to bring about the kingdom of God.

Explain how obeying the sixth and ninth commandments helps married people to love each other more.

How can you help your family to grow in faithfulness to one another?

OUR CATHOLIC FAITH

- Loving God, bless all married couples with the gift of faithful love.

- Why do you think it is important to respect one's own body and the bodies of others?

Called to Faithfulness

God helps married people to be faithful to each other in the sacrament of Matrimony. Matrimony is one of the two sacraments of service.

During the celebration of the sacrament of Matrimony, the priest and all present pray that the couple's love will stay strong so they can remain faithful forever.

In the families that parents create through their marriage, we learn the meaning of true and faithful love. We learn that we, too, are called to be faithful to our family, to ourselves, and to God's law.

As a member of a family, we have a responsibility to do our part to build up a loving community. We need to show our parents and our brothers and sisters how much we love them. Every day we should do all that we can to help our family to be happy.

Besides being faithful to our family, God also asks us to be faithful to ourselves. We do this when we love ourselves because we are made in God's image. Loving ourselves means respecting our bodies by what we say and think and do.

When we obey the sixth and ninth commandments, we also follow the teaching of Jesus. In the Beatitudes Jesus said, "Blessed are the clean of heart, for they will see God" (Matthew 5:8). Purity of heart reminds us to keep our attention always on Christ, whose love for us never ends.

Marriage Vows

A *marriage vow* is a promise that lasts forever. The man and woman being married promise to love each other in good times and in bad, in sickness and in health, until death.

Choose one part of the marriage vows (for example: "in good times and in bad"). Write what you think this might mean to a husband and wife.

_____

_____

_____

_____

We remember that every part of our body is good. We do not do anything to our body or to another person's body that is disrespectful in thought or word or action.

We do not read books or see movies that dishonor our bodies. We do not allow anyone to do anything to us that would dishonor our bodies. Our bodies are a wonderful gift from God, made for true and faithful love in marriage.

What are some of the ways that you are called to be faithful?

What will you do today to show your family that you love them?

163

OUR CATHOLIC FAITH

- Loving God, faithful One, help us to learn the true meaning of love.

- What can you do right now to grow as a faithful friend?

Living the Commandments

It takes a long time to learn how to love and be loved. If you learn what true love is now, someday it will be easier for you to keep your promise to love another person in marriage.

Learning to be faithful friends is a good way to learn about love. You want your friends to be loyal, and you want to be loyal to them. This is true friendship.

You keep the sixth and ninth commandments in many ways. You love someone when you share your time with that person. You listen to and talk with each other.

Friendship also means that you give up what you want for what the friend wants when it is good for your friend. You try to be patient with your friends when they get on your nerves. You remember that no one is perfect, that everyone has faults and shortcomings.

Some people may think that the sixth and ninth commandments are only for older people. But God wants young people to live these commandments in their own way. Guided by the Holy Spirit and the teachings of the Church, all people are to live these commandments in thought, word, and deed.

The Banns of Marriage

The Catholic Church teaches that marriage is a sacrament between a baptized man and woman. This means that it is a way of holiness for men and women and a gift of God. It also means that marriage is a gift to the whole Church. This is why marriage is celebrated in public with witnesses, not in private.

Catholics who want to be married meet with their parish priest. He helps them to prepare to celebrate the sacrament. He also may publish what is known as the *banns of marriage.*

The word *banns* means the public announcement of a future marriage. Usually the announcement of a couple's marriage is published in the parish bulletin or newspaper. Sometimes their names are read out at Mass. In this way, the whole Church family knows when its members are about to be married. The banns are normally published or announced for three weeks before the wedding ceremony.

Find out if and how the banns of marriage are posted in your parish. When you see or hear the banns, pray that the couples being married will be faithful marriage partners for their entire lives.

Banns of Marriage

I Anna Ortiz and Jorge Santiago

II Tai Chun and Lu Kwan

III Virginia Martin and Thomas Nadramia

Learn by heart **Faith Summary**

- The sixth commandment is "You shall not commit adultery." The ninth commandment is "You shall not covet your neighbor's wife."

- We do not do anything to our own body or to another person's body that is disrespectful in thought or word or action.

- To be faithful means to be loyal and true to someone.

Coming To Faith

Think of ways we can keep the sixth and ninth commandments right now in our lives. Role-play the following situations together.

Your older sister has gotten into trouble at school. Your parents are upset and are arguing with each other before dinner. You. . . .

One of your friends has a magazine with pictures you know you should not be looking at. Your friend tells you not to be a baby. You. . . .

Practicing Faith

You are not yet ready to promise to be faithful to someone in marriage for life. But you *are* ready to be faithful to promises, loyal to family and friends, and respectful of your own body and the bodies of other people.

Share your ideas by completing each statement.

- *Faithful* means. . . .

- I can be faithful to my family by. . . .

- I can be a faithful friend by. . . .

- I can be faithful to myself by. . . .

Make up a group prayer about being faithful. Pray it together.

Talk with your teacher about ways you and your family might use the "Faith Alive" section. Pray the Family Prayer with your teacher and friends.

REVIEW ■ TEST

Circle the letter beside the correct answer.

1. The sixth commandment is

  a. You shall not covet your neighbor's wife.

  b. You shall not commit adultery.

  c. You shall not lie.

2. To be faithful means to be

  a. friendly.

  b. loyal and true.

  c. sacred.

3. The ninth commandment is

  a. You shall not covet your neighbor's wife.

  b. You shall not commit adultery.

  c. You shall not lie.

4. Matrimony is a sacrament of

  a. service.

  b. healing.

  c. initiation.

5. How will you try to be a faithful friend?

_____

_____

FAITH ALIVE AT HOME AND IN THE PARISH

In this chapter your fourth grader learned the sixth and ninth commandments. It is never too early to lay a foundation for faithful adult love by teaching children how to be faithful to God, to oneself, to family, to friends, and to promises made. It is imperative that parents teach their children that sexuality is a great and beautiful gift of God's love.

When we truly cherish our bodies as temples of the Holy Spirit, we help young people to live the sixth and ninth commandments. Help them to see that the teachings of the Church will be a sure guide to a life of faithful and unselfish love.

Encourage your fourth grader to tell you immediately whether anyone suggests dishonoring or attempts to dishonor his or her body.

† Family Prayer

Pray this psalm prayer together with your family.

O God, you know me.
You know everything I do.
You created every part of me.
Guide me in your way.
Based on Psalm 139: 1, 2, 13, 24

18 Sharing Our Things
The Seventh and Tenth Commandments

Dear God, help us to share with people who are in need.

Our Life

Luke was crazy about planes. He made models and sometimes went to air shows with his dad. He made a beautiful model for his school's science fair. He was very proud of it until a classmate brought in a remote control plane and showed how it could fly.

Luke had never been so envious in his life. How he wanted that plane! He knew it was far too expensive for his family to afford.

After the fair, Luke saw the plane and the remote control in the classroom. No one was near. He could take the plane. Who would know? Luke had never stolen anything before. But he wanted that plane so much!

Finish the story. What did Luke do? Have you ever wanted something that was not yours? What is the best way to fight such a temptation?

Sharing Life

Discuss these questions together.

Why is it wrong to steal?

What do you think God wants us to do when we are tempted to steal?

What do you think God wants us to do when others do not have the things they need to live?

Use a large piece of drawing paper. Draw a cartoon figure with a dialogue "balloon" over its head. In the balloon print the question: "If God made enough for everyone in the world, why are so many people starving?"

Draw a second figure beside the first. In its dialogue balloon, write your response or reaction to that question.

Share your cartoons. Are your responses similar? different? Maybe you will have another response at the end of this chapter.

I think . . .

I think . . .

I think . . .

If God made enough for everyone in the world, why are so many people starving?

We Will Learn

- The seventh and tenth commandments teach us not to steal or damage what belongs to another.

- We live these commandments by not stealing and by sharing our things with others.

- We must always choose to obey the seventh and tenth commandments.

OUR CATHOLIC FAITH

■ God, giver of all gifts, teach us to be generous.

■ Why do you think it is wrong to take something that belongs to someone else?

Learning to Share

God told the first created people to care for his gift of creation. We are responsible for everything in our environment. We are to share God's gifts in creation with others.

We do God's will when we help people to have enough food and clothing. God wants all people to be treated fairly and justly. Everyone must have an equal chance for an education, a job with fair pay, enough food, and a decent place to live.

Since the beginning of human history, some people have been selfish and greedy and have not wanted to share. At times they even have wanted to steal their neighbors' possessions.

That is why God gave us the seventh and tenth commandments. The seventh commandment is "You shall not steal" (Exodus 20:15). The tenth commandment is "You shall not covet your neighbor's house . . . nor anything else that belongs to him" (Deuteronomy 5:21).

Each time we steal, we break God's commandment. We have no right to take or damage or destroy what belongs to another, even if we know we will not be caught. We must also share our things with people less fortunate than we are.

One day a rich man asked Jesus, "Good teacher, what must I do to inherit eternal life?"

Jesus told the man to obey the commandments. But the man said he had done that since he was young.

When Jesus heard this, he said to him, "There is still one thing left for you: sell all that you have and distribute it to the poor, and you will have a treasure in heaven. Then come, follow me."

Based on Luke 18:18–22

There are some people in the Church who have done exactly what Jesus asked the man to do. But Jesus does not call everyone to do this. It is a special calling, or vocation, in the Church. However, Jesus does want all of his disciples to be "poor in spirit." This means that possessions should never become the most important things in our lives. They are gifts from God that we must share with others.

The story of Jesus and the rich man also shows us that we are doing God's will when we share with the poor and needy and work for justice. As Jesus' faithful disciples who are poor in spirit, we are helping to bring about God's kingdom of justice and peace for all.

What do you learn from the story of the rich man about living the seventh and tenth commandments?

How can you live the advice of Jesus to be "poor in spirit"?

OUR CATHOLIC FAITH

■ Jesus, help us to understand that when we have you, we have everything.

■ Why do you think we should respect the rights of others?

Respecting Others' Rights

The first Christians learned from Jesus how to do God's loving will for us. They would sell their possessions and distribute the money according to the needs of all. Today the Catholic Church challenges us to be faithful to Jesus' teachings. How wonderful it would be if all people had what they needed and were treated fairly and justly. When we help others to have what they need, we are helping to bring about God's kingdom of justice and peace.

The seventh and tenth commandments remind us not to do the following on purpose:

- steal things from others, or borrow things without permission;
- deliberately break or destroy other people's property;
- cheat on tests or take the schoolwork of another;
- damage, write on, or paint on anyone's property;
- fail to take care of our possessions;
- be greedy and selfish about the things that are ours;
- be unfair or cheat others out of what is rightfully theirs.

Sometimes adults do things at their jobs that are against the seventh and tenth commandments:

- They steal things from the workplace or use the telephone all the time without permission to make personal calls. They are careless in their work or do not work for the time they are paid to work.
- Employers do not respect their workers when they pay them unjustly or do not give them clean and safe workplaces.

When all of us respect others and their belongings, we make the world a better place. We show we are living for God's kingdom.

FAITH WORD

Greed is wanting more than one's fair share or not wishing to share one's good fortune with others.

Explain to a friend or younger child the Christian attitude toward these problems.

Problem	Why it is sinful
greed	
stealing	
cheating	
damaging property	

- Is there anything in these lists that you never thought of as being wrong? Explain.

- How will you try to avoid doing these things?

OUR CATHOLIC FAITH

- Loving God, help us to accept the challenge of your commandments with faith and courage.

- Imagine a world without stealing. What would it be like?

Living the Commandments

The seventh and tenth commandments are God's laws. God gave them to us to help us be free to live together in justice and peace. These commandments teach us to respect the possessions and property of others and not to steal.

They also teach us to care for the good things of this world and not to be jealous, or envious, of what others have. Envy is one of the sins against the seventh and tenth commandments.

When we respect other people and choose not to take what is theirs, we are following Jesus' example and are doing God's will.

These commandments also remind us of the importance of work. We are not to be lazy and let everyone else take care of things for us. Each one of us has been given gifts and talents by God. How sad it is when people do not use their gifts or do not let these gifts develop and grow.

Jesus knew what a challenge we would have in living the seventh and tenth commandments. During his life, he gave us the best example. By the help and guidance of the Holy Spirit and through the teachings of the Church, we can live God's laws, too.

Supporting the Church

From the earliest times, Christians have supported the work of the Church through contributions. In his letters, Saint Paul often thanked the people for the money they had given him to carry on Christ's work.

Today Catholics continue to help carry on Christ's work by contributing to parish collections. Usually these collections are taken up at Mass during the Preparation of the Gifts. The collection reminds us that we offer ourselves to God as part of our worship.

The money we offer is used to pay salaries for the parish staff and to provide what is needed to run the parish—even for the bread and wine used at Mass.

Other kinds of collections are taken up during the year. Sometimes we have food and clothing collections for the needy. We also collect money to help run the diocese and to support the many works of charity that the Church does throughout the world.

The Church depends on each of us. That is why it is important for each Catholic to be as generous as possible in support of the Church. How can you begin now to be generous in your support of the Church?

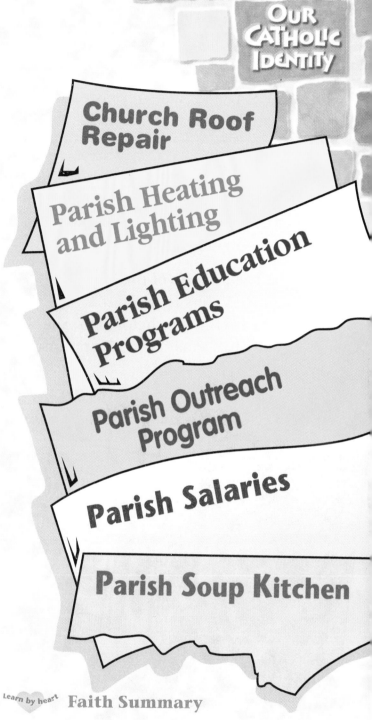

Church Roof Repair

Parish Heating and Lighting

Parish Education Programs

Parish Outreach Program

Parish Salaries

Parish Soup Kitchen

Learn by heart **Faith Summary**

- The seventh commandment is "You shall not steal." The tenth commandment is "You shall not covet your neighbor's house . . . ."

- We are responsible for God's gift of creation.

- We must share with people less fortunate than ourselves.

COMING TO FAITH

What would you say to each person in the following stories?

Jon and his friends like to spray paint pictures and words on walls and storefronts. "It's fun," he says, "and we never get caught."

"Everyone cheats," Dana says. "The teacher can't watch all of us. Besides, I'm getting good grades. Who gets hurt?"

Meg sees the pictures of the homeless families on TV. She tells you that she cannot do anything to help them. She says, "They live so far away. It's not my problem."

For the Needy

PRACTICING FAITH

Here is a very real and practical way to keep the seventh and tenth commandments. Decide what you can do together to help homeless children. Write your ideas below, then share them and come up with a group plan.

_____

_____

_____

_____

Talk with your teacher about ways you and your family might use the "Faith Alive" section. Encourage your family to do the family sharing activity. Close by praying the Our Father with your teacher and friends.

REVIEW · TEST

Circle the letter beside the correct answer.

1. The seventh commandment teaches us not to

   a. lie.

   b. kill.

   c. commit adultery.

   d. steal.

2. God created us to

   a. share our good things.

   b. avoid the homeless.

   c. take what belongs to others.

   d. keep what we have for ourselves.

3. The tenth commandment teaches us not to want to take our neighbor's

   a. wife or husband.

   b. possessions.

   c. life.

   d. name.

4. Greed is

   a. promising someone money.

   b. wanting more than one's share.

   c. showing disrespect.

   d. treating someone unfairly.

5. How will you show you respect school property?

_____

_____

FAITH ALIVE AT HOME AND IN THE PARISH

In this chapter your fourth grader has learned about the seventh and the tenth commandments. These commandments teach us to respect the possessions of others and the right of others to justice and equality. In addition, they remind us to care for the good things God has given us. These commandments reflect the profound social responsibility that our Christian faith gives us to act justly.

We live in a world that can be called a "throw-away" society. Young people need to learn not to waste things. If they follow the example of Jesus and the teachings of the Church, they will learn to value the rights of others and to have the right perspective on material goods and possessions. In this way they will never make these things the center of their lives.

Family Sharing

God has blessed us with many good things. This week, decide how your family can share some of its things with others. On a large piece of paper, write on one side, "Things we can share." Then write on the other side, "Persons with whom we can share." Have your family help you to make out a list. Decide on one thing you will share this week.

19 Living and Telling the Truth
The Eighth Commandment

O God, make us true and sincere in all we say and do.

OUR LIFE

Once upon a time an emperor ordered a set of new clothes. The tailors did not want the emperor to punish them because the clothes they made were not beautiful enough. So they pretended to have special material that only "intelligent" people could see; ordinary people could not see it because it was really invisible. The emperor believed their story and asked them to make robes for him out of this wonderful material.

When the tailors said the robes were finished, the emperor "wore" them in a parade. The people, afraid to offend the emperor, shouted, "How beautiful the emperor's new robes are!" But a small child cried, "Mother, the emperor has no clothes!"

Why did everyone pretend to see the emperor's new robes?

Do you sometimes find it hard to tell the truth? Tell about it.

SHARING LIFE

Discuss these questions together. Why do people sometimes tell lies?

How can telling and living the truth help us to be free?

178

Make a list of times when people are tempted to tell a lie. Share your lists together and discuss ways to be more truthful. For example:

It is **easy** to lie when . . .

_____

_____

_____

_____

I should say . . .

_____

_____

_____

_____

This week we will learn how harmful lies and gossip can be.

We Will Learn

- The eighth commandment requires that we tell and live the truth.

- This commandment teaches that it is wrong to lie, to gossip, to tell another person's secrets.

- We choose to be God's truthful people.

179

OUR CATHOLIC FAITH

Lord Jesus, you are the way, the truth, and the life. Help us to follow you.

Is it always easy to tell the truth? Why or why not?

God Calls Us to Be Truthful

God told the people of Israel that as his own people, they must always tell and live the truth. The eighth commandment that God gave Moses was "You shall not bear false witness against your neighbor" (Exodus 20:16). This means we are not to lie.

To lie means not to tell the truth. God wants us to speak the truth about ourselves and others. He also wants us to live the truth at all times. We live the truth by always doing his loving and life-giving will for us. Doing God's will brings us true freedom.

God knows that it is not easy for us to be truthful. That is why we must ask the Holy Spirit for the courage to be the kind of people God wants us to be.

In the Bible, we read what it means to be a truthful person.

Whoever walks without blame
  doing what is right,
    speaking truth from the heart;
Who does not slander a neighbor,
  does no harm to another,
    never defames a friend.

Psalm 15:2–3

Jesus always lived the truth in what he said and did. He told us, "If you remain in my word, you will truly be my disciples, and you will know the truth, and the truth will set you free" (John 8:31–32). When we live as disciples of Jesus, full of love, we are God's truthful people. To live the truth as disciples of Jesus is the best kind of freedom.

Jesus showed us how to be truthful, even when being truthful was difficult. On the night before he died, Jesus was arrested and brought before Pontius Pilate, a Roman official in Palestine. Pilate asked Jesus whether he was a king.

Jesus said to him, "You say I am a king. For this I was born and for this I came into the world, to testify to the truth. Everyone who belongs to the truth listens to my voice."
John 18:37

How do we listen to Jesus? Jesus gave us the Church to teach us the truth and to help us share that truth with others. Guided by the Holy Spirit, Catholics are called to witness to their faith and share it with the world. This is the faith that we profess each Sunday at Mass. We do this at the Profession of Faith when we recite the creed.

Living as true disciples of Jesus means that we obey the eighth commandment and live the truths of our faith. When we do this in word and in action, we can bring about true justice and true peace in the world.

PONTIUS PILATE

Pontius Pilate was a Roman official in the land where Jesus lived. He was appointed by the Roman emperor.

- How can telling the truth set you free to be a strong disciple of Jesus?

- What will you do today to be a more truthful person?

OUR CATHOLIC FAITH

■ Loving God, give us understanding hearts so that our words may never hurt others.

■ Should we always tell the truth about someone—no matter what? Explain.

A Truthful People

We obey the eighth commandment when we speak the truth.

One day Jesus said to his disciples, "From the fullness of the heart the mouth speaks" (Matthew 12:34). This means that people show how they really feel by the things they say.

If we are trying to be like Jesus, we will have hearts full of love and compassion. We will be God's truthful people.

If our hearts are not filled with love, then we will speak unkindly and sometimes even lie. If we tell the truth, people will know they can trust us. This helps our families and neighborhoods to be communities of justice and peace.

Sometimes we lie about things we have done. We may not want to take responsibility for our actions. We may be afraid of being punished. At other times we lie or exaggerate about something we have or can do. We want others to think we are important, or "big shots."

Sometimes we lie about other people. Maybe we are jealous of them or do not like them. We make up a story that makes them look bad. We harm people each time we spread a lie about them.

We can also hurt someone by telling things about which we should be silent. This happens when we gossip or tell **private** or **secret** things about someone, things that would hurt that person if others found out. The eighth commandment teaches us that it is wrong to use even the truth to hurt others. Anyone who destroys another person's reputation must repair the **damage** done.

On the other hand, people might ask us to keep a secret about something bad that they are doing. We should not promise to keep such secrets. We need to speak to a parent, a teacher, or a priest, because keeping such secrets can hurt people.

If someone is drinking or taking drugs, he or she needs help. Keeping this a secret can lead the one who is doing something so harmful into serious trouble. In such cases, it is far more loving to tell the truth to someone who can help.

A person who has the courage to tell and live the truth is a true follower of Jesus Christ. Such a person will also have the courage to speak out and live for God's kingdom of justice and peace.

Are there some secrets we should not keep? Tell why.

Will you ask the Holy Spirit for the courage always to tell and live the truth?

OUR CATHOLIC FAITH

Come, Holy Spirit, give us the courage we need to be truthful.

Describe what living the truth means to you. Give examples.

Choosing to Be Truthful

We can always choose to be truthful, no matter how difficult it is. The Holy Spirit helps us to tell the truth.

We must tell the truth, even when we are tempted to lie in order to:

- avoid being punished for an accident, a mistake, or something we did wrong;

- get someone into trouble;

- make ourselves look important;

- get more of something than we deserve.

The choice is ours. If we ask, God the Holy Spirit will always give us the courage we need to be truthful. The Holy Spirit will help us follow the way of Jesus, who said, "I am the way and the truth and the life" (John 14:6).

After learning more about the eighth commandment, we see that all Ten Commandments are part of God's truth to us, the truth that God wants us to know and live.

The first psalm in the Bible tells us about those who really understand and live God's law in their lives.

The law of the LORD is their joy;
God's law they study day
and night.
They are like a tree
planted near streams of water,
that yields its fruit in
season;
Its leaves never
wither;
whatever they do prospers.

Based on Psalm 1:2–3

Witnesses to the Truth

All during the year, Catholics celebrate the memory of men and women who gave up their lives for the truth of the Christian faith. We call these brave and courageous people martyrs. The word martyr means "witness," and a witness is someone who tells the truth either in word or in action.

When the Church began, there were many people who did not like or understand the disciples of Jesus Christ. Often the early Christians were persecuted and even put to death for their faith. When this happened, the Church remembered the words of Jesus from the Beatitudes: "Blessed are they who are persecuted . . . for theirs is the kingdom of heaven."

The stories of the martyrs are stories of great faith and courage. You may wish to learn more about the stories of the apostles and first disciples, many of whom were martyred for their faith in Jesus Christ. You can also read about other early martyrs such as Saint Lucy, Saint Cecilia, and Saint Agnes.

Martyrs are not just people from the past, however. Christians are still persecuted for their faith today. You may want to read more about the lives of modern martyrs such as Archbishop Oscar Romero and the four courageous women who died in the country of El Salvador doing missionary work.

Father Miguel Pro, Mexican Jesuit, executed for the faith, 1927.

Jean Donovan, American lay missionary, killed in El Salvador, 1980 for her faith.

Learn by heart **Faith Summary**

- The eighth commandment is "You shall not tell lies against your neighbor."

- This commandment teaches us that it is wrong to lie, to tell someone's secrets, or to gossip.

- A person who has the courage to tell and live the truth is a true disciple of Jesus Christ.

COMING TO FAITH

Knowing the eighth commandment, tell what you would do or what you would say to the people in these stories.

Justin has problems reading. After school he goes to special classes to learn to read better. One day at recess, Ryan tells you he found out that Justin has to go to the "slow class." Ryan wants to tell everyone. When you say it would be wrong, he answers, "Well, it's the truth, isn't it?"

Samantha tells you that she meets friends in the park each day. They give her pills that make her feel relaxed and happy. She asks you not to tell anyone.

Chris is very jealous of José, who is better in sports. One day, the principal announces that a gym window has been broken. Chris tells everyone that he saw José do it. This is not true, but now the whole school thinks José broke the window. Chris tells you that he was only fooling.

PRACTICING FAITH

Once a person spread harmful gossip and lies about someone. He told Saint Francis de Sales what he had done. Francis told him to empty a big feather pillow out the window and then gather up every feather. The person said this was impossible to do. The saint told him that it was just as impossible to restore the good reputation of the person lied about.

What will you do to be a more truthful person?

What will you do when you want to gossip? When you hear gossip?

Talk with your teacher about ways you and your family might use the "Faith Alive" section. You might find time to say the Family Prayer together. Pray it now with your teacher and friends.

REVIEW ■ TEST

Circle the letter beside the correct answer.

1. The eighth commandment is

   a. You shall not steal.

   b. You shall not commit adultery.

   c. You shall not tell lies.

   d. You shall not kill.

2. If we tell the truth, others will know they can

   a. trust us.

   b. fear us.

   c. avoid us.

   d. gossip about us.

3. We live the truth by

   a. avoiding being punished.

   b. making ourselves look important.

   c. doing God's will.

   d. not getting into trouble.

4. Who asked Jesus whether or not he was a king?

   a. Pontius Pilate

   b. Moses

   c. Peter

   d. John

5. What have you learned about the eighth commandment for your own life?

_____

_____

FAITH ALIVE AT HOME AND IN THE PARISH

In this chapter on the eighth commandment, your fourth grader learned that God calls us to be truthful with others, both in our words and in our actions. We are called to correct any falsehood we may have started so as to protect the reputation of others.

Telling the truth demonstrates our concern for others, our love for our neighbor. It enables us to know the true freedom of God's children who are guided by the Spirit of truth. Jesus himself tells us, "If you remain in my word, you will truly be my disciples and you will know the truth, and the truth will set you free" (John 8:31–32). Make truth-telling a major value in your family.

† Family Prayer

O God, help us to be:
A family who obeys God in everything
   and always does what is right,
whose words are true and sincere,
   and who does not spread lies
     about others.
A family who does no wrong to friends
   and does not spread rumors about
     neighbors.

20 Preparing for Lent

Our Life

Once there was a little caterpillar who thought she was the ugliest creature in the whole world. She was fuzzy and green. When she looked at her reflection in a puddle of water, she saw her six tiny eyes, six tiny legs, and all that fuzzy hair.

One day she curled up and went to sleep. As she slept, many changes took place.

After many weeks, the little caterpillar woke up. She found herself surrounded by a warm, soft cocoon. She pushed and pushed until the side of the cocoon broke open. Then she pulled herself out.

She looked in a puddle of water and saw the reflection of a beautiful butterfly. "Oh," thought the little caterpillar, "look how beautiful that butterfly is! It has two beautiful wings of blue and gold." The little caterpillar sighed and thought, "Oh, how I wish I looked like that." She was so sad.

As she raised her little caterpillar foot to wipe away her tears, she thought, "What's this?" A beautiful blue and gold wing had moved in front of her eyes. "It's me!" she realized. "I've turned into a beautiful butterfly!"

Then the butterfly, which had once been the ugliest caterpillar in the world, began to fly. She flew from flower to flower.

How do you think the butterfly felt?

Sharing Life

Discuss these questions together.

How can people change to make their lives more beautiful?

What changes can you make right now?

How does Jesus want us to change?

Look in an encyclopedia or magazines for pictures of different kinds of butterflies. Draw and color your favorite. Cut out your drawing. Write your name on it and what you hope to do this Lent. Then string your butterfly on thin wire with those of your friends. Hang the butterflies where the air will make them move.

When you look at the butterflies during this season of Lent, remember that God is calling us to change what we need to change in ourselves.

Diane
I will …

Rafael
I will …

We Will Learn

- Lent is a time of change and growth.
- During Lent, we remember the promises made at Baptism.
- We prepare for Easter by prayer, fasting, and good works.

A Time for Change

The season of Lent is a time of change and growth. It is like springtime, when cocoons burst open and flowers begin to bud. It is a time for new beginnings. We try even harder to grow in our Catholic faith and to be better disciples of Jesus Christ. We prepare for the greatest celebration of the Church year, Easter.

During Lent we remember the promises of Baptism. We join in a special way with those who are preparing to be baptized at Easter and those who will receive the other sacraments of initiation, Confirmation and Eucharist.

Lent is a time for improving the way all of us live as God's people. We have to learn to be generous. Jesus told his disciples, "Whoever wishes to come after me must deny himself, take up his cross, and follow me."

Matthew 16:24

Jesus wanted the people to know that he was calling them to live as God's people. He told them: "The kingdom of God is at hand. Repent, and believe in the gospel."

Mark 1:15

Jesus brought us God's love and life. He offered up his life for the whole world and won for us the new life of his resurrection. Jesus brought us life that lasts **forever**.

A Time for Preparation

Each year during Lent, we prepare to celebrate Jesus' resurrection by remembering his life and death. We remember that it was through his death that Jesus entered into his resurrection and won new life for us.

As we prepare ourselves during the forty days of Lent, we remember that we have become part of Jesus' death and resurrection. By our Baptism, we have died to sin and have been given God's own life in Jesus Christ.

We prepare for Easter in many ways—by doing good works and by praying especially for those who will be baptized at Easter. We try to change the way we live our lives, even though we might fail from time to time. But always we continue to try and be better Catholics.

- We make sacrifices when we give things up. Lent is a good time for giving up things we do not need—for example, candy or watching TV.

- We do good works when we help other people. Many people give the money they save on candy and snacks to help the needy. Some people do this all year long.

- We take extra time for prayer during Lent. We pray the stations of the cross or the rosary every week.

Coming To Faith

Everyone has something hard or sad to face in life. Nothing is as difficult as the cross that Jesus had to bear. Still some things in life can be difficult for us. What is your difficult cross to bear? Perhaps it is an illness. Perhaps you have trouble at home or with friends. Maybe you have a problem that is keeping you from being your best self.

What do you think Jesus meant when he said that his followers should carry their cross and follow him?

Write how you can try to carry your cross this Lent.

_____

_____

Practicing Faith
A Lenten Celebration

Opening Song

Sing to the tune of "Kumbayah."

Lent is a time to change and grow.
Here we are Lord, help us know,
How to be your disciples true.
Oh, Jesus, we follow you.

Opening Prayer

All: Jesus, this Lent, help us grow in our love of you and others. Help us to grow in the new life you have given us.

Reader: A reading from the book of the prophet Hosea (2:23–25).
"On that day I will respond,
    says the LORD;
I will respond to the heavens,
and they shall respond to the earth;
The earth shall respond to the grain,
    and wine, and oil, . . .
I will say . . . 'You are my people'".

The word of the Lord.

All: Thanks be to God.

Reader: A reading from the holy gospel according to John (12:24, 26).
Jesus says, "unless a grain of wheat falls to the ground and dies, it remains just a grain of wheat; but if it dies, it produces much fruit. . . .Whoever serves me must follow me. . . ."

The gospel of the Lord.

All: Praise to you, Lord Jesus Christ.

Prayer Action

Leader: You will receive a seed and a cup filled with dirt. As you plant the seed, listen to these words. Think how you want to prepare yourself during Lent to share in Jesus' new life.

Jesus, you said that unless a seed dies, it does not produce other seeds. During Lent, Jesus, help me to "die" to:

- being selfish;
- saying things that hurt others;
- doing things that hurt others;
- being unfair to others.

Jesus, help your new life to grow in me so that I may:

- become more loving;
- care for others;
- say and do loving things;
- be a peacemaker.

Closing Hymn

Sing to the tune of "Kumbayah."

Jesus, help us to prepare
And please lead us to be aware
Of your new life that grows in us.
Loving Jesus, we do trust.

Talk with your teacher about ways you and your family might use the "Faith Alive" section. You might want to plan a time for you and a family member to pray a special Lenten prayer together each day

REVIEW ▪ TEST

Fill in the blanks to complete the statements.

1. There are _____ days in Lent.

2. During Lent, we prepare for the celebration of

_____.

3. We are given a share in God's own life in the sacrament

of _____.

4. During Lent we try harder to become better _____ of Jesus Christ.

5. Jesus said that we must carry our cross and follow him. How can someone your age do that?

_____

_____

FAITH ALIVE AT HOME AND IN THE PARISH

This lesson deepened your fourth grader's understanding of Lent as a time to prepare for Easter. Lent is a time of spiritual renewal, of preparation for the sacraments of initiation by the catechumens of our parish. Through prayer, fasting, and good works, we reflect on the meaning of our lives and on the salvation that the suffering, death, and resurrection of Jesus gained for us.

The Lenten Scripture readings help us focus on our baptismal promise to reject sin and to live as disciples of Jesus Christ. We are challenged to review the patterns of our lives that are sinful and to renew our commitment to change our lives.

We remember that by being baptized into the passion, death, and resurrection of Jesus, we have been made sharers in God's own life.

Learn by heart **Faith Summary**

- Lent is a time of preparation for Easter.

- We prepare for Easter by prayer, fasting, and good works.

21 Celebrating Easter

OUR LIFE

An Easter Play

Narrator: As our play begins, two people are walking together down a dusty road.

First Person: I never thought it would happen. Everyone loved Jesus so much.

Second Person: I know what you mean. I couldn't believe it when they told me that Jesus had been arrested.

First Person: Did you see him when they made him carry the cross?

Second Person: I kept thinking that something would happen, that someone would say, "Stop! Jesus should not be crucified!"

First Person: I heard him say, "Father, forgive them, they know not what they do" as they raised him on the cross. (Luke 23:34)

Second Person: But now he is with us again. He has risen from the dead as he promised!

First Person: Many of my friends have already seen him. Some of them have sat at table with him and saw him break the bread.

Narrator: The friends of Jesus returned to their homes in Jerusalem. There they found the disciples of Jesus together. Everyone was saying:

All: Jesus is risen! Jesus is risen! Alleluia!

SHARING LIFE

What did you learn from Jesus' two friends?

Why is Easter so important to Christians?

Why should we be happy at Easter?

Look at the things the disciples in the Easter play are saying about Jesus. Work with a partner to write something else they might remember about him. For example:

- "Do you remember the time he calmed the storm at sea?"

- "Do you remember when he brought the daughter of Jairus back to life?"

Now with the group choose parts and act out the Easter play.

Add your own remembrances to the play right after the **First Person's** opening lines. Then continue the play to the end.

We Will Learn

- The Easter season lasts from Easter to Pentecost Sunday.

- For fifty days after Easter we celebrate the resurrection of Jesus.

- The risen Christ is with us today.

Our Catholic Faith

The Easter Triduum

All during Lent, we have been preparing to celebrate the most important time of the Church year, the Easter Triduum. Through our prayer, fasting, and good works, we are ready to remember the death and resurrection of our Lord and Savior, Jesus Christ.

Lent ends on Thursday of Holy Week. Then the Catholic Church gathers to celebrate the Triduum. The word *Triduum* means "three days." The Triduum begins on Holy Thursday with the Evening Mass of the Lord's Supper. It continues through Good Friday and Holy Saturday, and it ends with Evening Prayer on Easter Sunday.

At the Mass on Holy Thursday evening, we recall all that Jesus did at the Last Supper. We give thanks for the gift of the Eucharist and remember what Jesus taught us about serving others when he washed the feet of his apostles.

On Good Friday, we gather in the afternoon at a special liturgy to remember the passion and death of Jesus on the cross.

On Holy Saturday night, we begin and gather in darkness to celebrate the Easter Vigil. The word *vigil* means "keeping watch." We are watching for Christ our Light.

During the Easter Vigil liturgy, we bless the new fire and paschal candle, reminding us of the risen Christ. We hear God's word and then bless the baptismal water. We welcome new members into the Church community and celebrate new life through the sacraments of initiation and the renewal of baptismal promises.

The Easter Season

For fifty days after Easter we celebrate the resurrection of Jesus and our new life in him. This is the Easter season. It lasts from Easter to Pentecost Sunday.

Alleluia is the Christian song of Easter joy. It means "praise God" and expresses our great happiness at Jesus' victory over death and his risen presence with us.

Learn to sing the Easter Alleluia with your parish. Decorate the word here.

COMING TO FAITH

What is the most important time of the Church year?

_____

What do we remember at Easter?

_____

_____

The Easter candle is a symbol of the risen Christ, the Light of the World.

197

PRACTICING FAITH

An Easter Prayer

Opening Hymn

Sing an Easter Alleluia.

Leader: Jesus Christ is the Light of the World. At Eastertime, let us thank Jesus for being with us always.

All: Jesus is risen, alleluia! All praise and glory to Christ our Light!

Leader: Bread that is grown from seeds in the ground becomes the Body of Christ. Grapes that are grown from seeds in the ground become the Blood of Christ.

Reader 1: Blessed are you, Lord, God of all creation. Through your goodness we have this bread to offer.

Reader 2: Blessed are you, Lord, God of all creation. Through your goodness we have this wine to offer.

All: Jesus, help us to recognize you when we take part in the Mass. During the Eucharistic prayer, help us to recognize you as your friends did after you rose from the dead.

Leader: Jesus Christ is the Light of the World. On this feast of Easter, let us thank Jesus for being with us always.

All: Jesus is risen, alleluia! All praise and glory to Christ our Light!

Closing Hymn

"Jesus Is Risen" (verse 2)

On this most holy day of days,
Let us together sing his praise!
Alleluia! Alleluia!
Raise joyful voices to the sky!
Sing out, ye heavens, in reply:

Alleluia! Alleluia! Alleluia!

Alleluia! Alleluia!

Talk with your teacher about ways you and your family might use the "Faith Alive" section. Share an Easter prayer with members of your family.

REVIEW ■ TEST

Fill in the blanks to complete the statements.

1. The Easter Triduum begins on _____ evening
and ends on Easter Sunday evening.

2. The word *Triduum* means _____.

3. On Holy Thursday we give thanks for the _____.

4. The Easter season extends from Easter to _____.

5. Christians are called to be "Easter people."
What does that mean to you?

_____

_____

_____

FAITH ALIVE AT HOME AND IN THE PARISH

In this chapter, your fourth grader learned more about Easter, especially the Easter Triduum. The resurrection of Jesus is the central truth of our faith handed on to us by the first Christians. Christ died for our sins to liberate us from the power of evil and to bring us new life. His resurrection is the pledge of our future glory—life forever with God.

This lesson provides the opportunity for you to deepen your child's awareness that the risen Christ is with us today in many ways, but especially in the Eucharist. Encourage your child to meet Christ there often and to recognize him as well in the poor, the hungry, and the homeless. As Jesus himself said, "whatever you did for one of these least brothers of mine, you did for me" (Matthew 25:40).

Learn by heart **Faith Summary**

● The Easter Triduum begins on Holy Thursday evening and ends on Easter Sunday evening.

● The Easter season includes the fifty days between Easter and Pentecost.

22 The Spirit Gives Us Life

OUR LIFE

Angela didn't want to see her Gram in the nursing home. She wanted things to be the way they used to be when Gram played games with her and drove her all over town.

She was afraid of seeing this Gram who now sat in a wheelchair and looked so feeble.

As Angela opened the door, she saw Gram sitting by the window. A tear trickled down her grandmother's cheek.

Angela was about to cry, too. Then she felt a surge of courage and a deep love for her Gram. She said in a clear voice, "Gram, I love you," and hugged her.

Where do you think Angela's new courage came from?

Who helps you to do difficult things? Explain.

There are many people in our lives who give us courage and strength in difficult times. Who are they?

What kind of power do these people give?

SHARING LIFE

Do you think that there is a power you cannot see or touch that helps people to do good? What is it?

Have you ever been given the power to make a hard decision? to do something brave? Tell about it.

Can you imagine times when God the Holy Spirit helps us to do difficult things?

Together with your group put some balloons into the air in your classroom. Imagine that these balloons stand for *life*. Stand in a circle and together try to keep the balloons afloat by blowing on them. (Use your hands only when they are really needed.)

After a few minutes, stop and ask yourselves:

- Was it easy to keep the balloons (life) from dropping?

- Could you have kept all the balloons afloat by yourself?

Suggest ways we can support God's life in one another. God gives us the power to do this, as we will learn in this chapter.

We Will Learn

- God the Holy Spirit is with us today.

- The Holy Spirit gives us life and special gifts.

- The Holy Spirit helps us to make right choices and to do God's will.

OUR CATHOLIC FAITH

- Come, Holy Spirit, guide the Church in love.
- How do you think people get the courage to make right decisions?

The Power of the Holy Spirit

Jesus knew that his disciples would need help to carry on his mission and to do God's loving will. That is why he promised to send the Holy Spirit to help them.

On Pentecost Sunday, God the Holy Spirit came upon Jesus' disciples. All of them were filled with the Holy Spirit. The gifts they received from the Spirit enabled them to go forth with courage to live for and preach Jesus' kingdom.

When new Christians were baptized, they, too, were filled with the Holy Spirit. The Holy Spirit helped them to live as true disciples of Jesus. They became known for their wonderful love and care for everyone.

The first Christians came together often to pray and to share the Eucharist. By the power of the Holy Spirit, Jesus was present with them in the Eucharist.

Because they were filled with the Holy Spirit, the first Christians were able to do some of the things Jesus had done.

One day two men went to Peter. They told him that Tabitha, a Christian woman, had died. Everyone in Tabitha's village loved her and was very upset. Tabitha had spent all her time doing good and helping the poor. All of her friends were waiting for Peter to return to the village with the two men.

God's will is what God wants us to do. We can call it God's "loving will" because he always wants what is best for us.

After praying, Peter called out, "Tabitha, get up!" Tabitha opened her eyes and sat up. Peter called her friends back into the room and presented Tabitha to them.

They were so happy that they spread the news about Tabitha throughout the whole area. Then many more people believed in Jesus.

Based on Acts of the Apostles 9:36–42

God the Holy Spirit, the third Person of the Blessed Trinity, is with us today. The Holy Spirit first comes to us when we are baptized. By the power of the Holy Spirit, we are freed from sin and made members of the body of Christ. Now we can choose not to sin and to live as disciples of Jesus.

The Holy Spirit will also come to you in a special way in the sacrament of Confirmation. In Confirmation, the Spirit will strengthen you to do God's loving will and to live for the kingdom, or reign, of God.

When Peter arrived at Tabitha's house, he was taken to her room. Her friends were standing around the bed, crying. Peter asked them to leave the room. Then he knelt down and prayed.

- What did you learn from the story of Tabitha?

- What will you do today to imitate her example of Christian living?

203

OUR CATHOLIC FAITH

God the Holy Spirit, fill us with your gifts.

Tell some ways the Holy Spirit helps you.

The Gifts of the Holy Spirit

It is not always easy to do God's will. We know that the Ten Commandments, the Law of Love, the Beatitudes, and the Spiritual and Corporal Works of Mercy can help us know the right things to do. But sometimes we are afraid to do the right thing, or we are confused about what is right and what is wrong.

That is why Jesus sends the Holy Spirit to each of us to be our Helper. Saint Paul tells us that God the Holy Spirit helps us make the right decision.

To help us, the Holy Spirit gives us special gifts. The Holy Spirit gives us these special gifts so that, like the disciples on the first Pentecost, we will have the courage we need to follow Jesus. Pages 204–205 name and explain these gifts of the Holy Spirit.

Study these pages so that you will understand the gifts that the Holy Spirit gives you in the sacrament of Confirmation.

God the Holy Spirit helps us to make good choices. Filled with the Holy Spirit, we can try each day to do God's loving will in all that we say and do. To help us do this, we should pray this prayer to the Holy Spirit often:

† Come, Holy Spirit, fill the hearts of your faithful and enkindle in them the fire of your love. Send forth your Spirit and they shall be created and you shall renew the face of the earth.

Wisdom

Gives us the power to know what God wants us to do. It helps us to make the decision God wants us to make.

Understanding

Helps us to see how Jesus wants us to live in our world today. It shows us how we can help stop injustice and unfairness.

The Gifts of the Holy Spirit

Right Judgment

Helps us to assist others in knowing what is right and how they can be courageous in doing it.

Courage

Helps us to do God's loving will, even when we are afraid.

Knowledge

Helps us to know our faith and what is needed to serve God.

Reverence

Helps us to show our love for God in all our thoughts, words, and actions.

Wonder and Awe

Helps us to put God first in our lives and to show respect for God's name, the holy name of Jesus, holy places and things.

Explain each gift of the Holy Spirit in your own words.

When will you pray for the help of the Holy Spirit?

OUR CATHOLIC FAITH

■ Holy Spirit, help us always to know and live the truth.

■ Which gift of the Holy Spirit do you need most at this time? Why?

The Holy Spirit Helps Us

Each of us needs the help of God the Holy Spirit to live as Jesus showed us. The Holy Spirit guides and directs the whole Church and each of us every day.

All leaders—those in the Church and those in every country in the world—need the Holy Spirit's guidance. Famous people and ordinary people need the help that the Holy Spirit gives.

The Holy Spirit guides and directs us to live as disciples of Jesus. The Holy Spirit is God's special gift to us. In the Bible we read that "the love of God has been poured out into our hearts through the holy Spirit that has been given to us" (Romans 5:5).

With God's love in our hearts, we can love others and do God's loving will.

Symbols for the Holy Spirit

The symbol for the Holy Spirit that is best known to most Catholics is the *dove*. Very often in our parish churches we see this symbol in stained-glass windows or in other works of art. The symbol reminds us of the gospel story of Jesus' baptism by John the Baptist in the Jordan River: Jesus saw the Spirit of God decending like a dove and coming upon him.

The dove is not the only symbol we use to remind us of the Holy Spirit, however. Another symbol is *fire* or a *flame*. When the Holy Spirit first came upon the disciples of Jesus after his resurrection, the Spirit was said to have come like small flames of fire (Based on Acts 2:3).

Sometimes the symbols of *cloud* and *light* are used to help us remember the Holy Spirit, too. Once when Jesus was with his apostles Peter, James, and John high on a mountaintop, he was transfigured, or changed, in a brilliant light before their eyes. A cloud came over them, and they heard God say that Jesus was God's own Son. You can read all about it in Luke 9:28–35.

The dove, fire, cloud, and light are just a few symbols for the Holy Spirit. Think for a moment. What beautiful symbol can you make to help remind yourself and others of God the Holy Spirit?

Learn by heart **Faith Summary**

- God the Holy Spirit fills each of us with special gifts.

- The gifts of the Holy Spirit are wisdom, understanding, right judgment, courage, knowledge, reverence, and wonder and awe.

- When we pray for guidance, God the Holy Spirit will help us to make the right choices.

Coming To Faith

Name the gift of the Holy Spirit that you think each of the following people used most. Tell why.

Jean Donovan was a lay missionary who left her home to help the poor in El Salvador. Jean went because she felt she could help people there. She was murdered because of her work with the poor. We call her a martyr for her faith.

Armando's mom is one of the most respected people in the neighborhood. When people are upset and need to make a decision, they talk with her.

Name a special gift you have received from the Holy Spirit. How do you use this gift?

Name a gift of the Holy Spirit you might need today. Tell why.

Practicing Faith

Tell what you can do this week with the help of the Holy Spirit at home, at school, or in your parish or neighborhood.

Pray together the prayer to the Holy Spirit on page 204. Then sing.

Come, Holy Spirit, Creator blest,
And in our hearts take up your rest.
Come with your grace and heavenly aid
To fill the hearts which you have made;
To fill the hearts which you have made.

Talk with your teacher about ways you and your family might use the "Faith Alive" section. Explain the gifts of the Holy Spirit to a family member and do the activity together.

REVIEW ▪ TEST

Match.

1. Courage

_____ gives us the power to make good decisions

2. Reverence

_____ what God wants us to do

3. Wisdom

_____ helps us do God's will even when afraid

4. God's will

_____ helps to assist others in knowing what is right

_____ helps us show love for God in all we do

5. Name a gift of the Holy Spirit you might need this week. How will you use it?

_____

_____

FAITH ALIVE AT HOME AND IN THE PARISH

Your fourth grader has learned that Jesus did not leave us alone. He sent us the Holy Spirit to be our Helper. God the Holy Spirit is the third Person of the Blessed Trinity.

Many Catholics have recently renewed their awareness of the central activity of the Holy Spirit in the Church and in their own lives. We can live the Christian life only by the power of God the Holy Spirit. The Holy Spirit moves us to pray, act, and live as Jesus' disciples. The Spirit challenges us to be alert to situations that demand our attention as Christian people. Prompted by the Spirit, we direct all of our prayers to the Father, our Creator, through the Son, our Redeemer, and in the Holy Spirit, our Sanctifier.

The Gifts of the Holy Spirit

Have your fourth grader write the names of the gifts of the Holy Spirit on slips of paper. Have each family member pick a gift and tell how he or she will ask God for it this week.

Encourage your fourth grader to make a pennant with the gift he or she chose printed on one side. On the other side is written how he or she will try to live that gift.

† Family Prayer

Pray at bedtime:

O come, Holy Spirit. Help me to be wise.
Help me to be kind, patient, and brave.
Help me to bring your peace, your justice,
your love, and your joy to those around me.
Amen.

23 The Church Guides Us

O Holy Spirit, thank you for guiding the Church in the way of Jesus Christ.

OUR LIFE

Here are some pictures of our Church at work in the world.

Tell what you see the Church doing.

Name other ways the Church works for Christ's kingdom in the world.

SHARING LIFE

Discuss these questions:

Imagine yourself in any of these pictures. What would you be doing?

Imagine ways that your parish needs your help. How can fourth graders serve the Church?

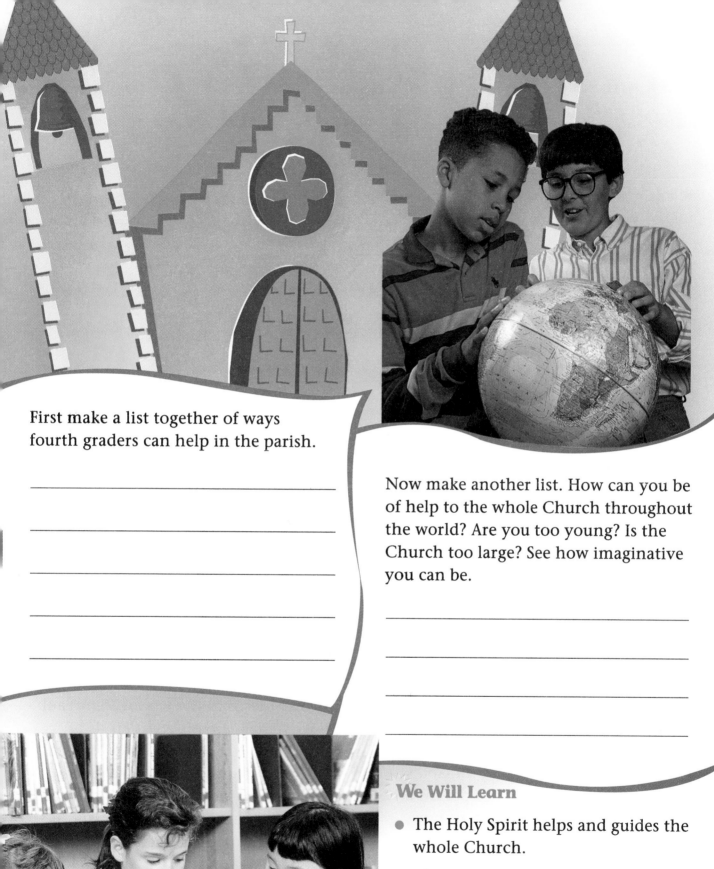

First make a list together of ways fourth graders can help in the parish.

_____

_____

_____

_____

_____

Now make another list. How can you be of help to the whole Church throughout the world? Are you too young? Is the Church too large? See how imaginative you can be.

_____

_____

_____

_____

We Will Learn

- The Holy Spirit helps and guides the whole Church.

- The Laws of the Church help us to live as good Catholics.

- In our parish we worship God and take part in the celebration of the sacraments.

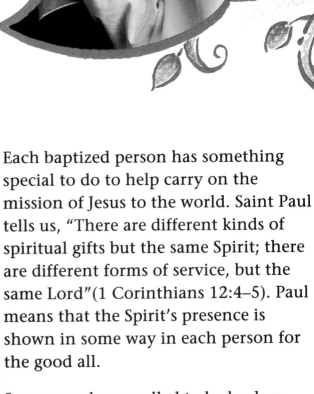

■ Lord Jesus, help us to carry on
your work in the world today.

■ Why is it important that we as
Christians offer guidance and
help to one another?

Our Church Guides Us

Jesus called his disciples to be his
Church and to carry on his mission
in the world. The risen Christ sent
the Holy Spirit to the disciples. The
Holy Spirit helped them to become
the body of Christ, the Church.

As members of the Church, we work
together in our parishes and with all
Catholics throughout the world. We
help one another to continue Jesus'
mission.

Today the Holy Spirit helps the Church
continue Jesus' mission of preaching
the good news and working for God's
kingdom. The Holy Spirit guides the
pope and bishops, who teach us how
to carry on Jesus' work. They remind
us that everyone in the Church must
work for the kingdom of God. The
Holy Spirit helps the whole Church to
do this and gives special gifts to each
one of us.

Each baptized person has something
special to do to help carry on the
mission of Jesus to the world. Saint Paul
tells us, "There are different kinds of
spiritual gifts but the same Spirit; there
are different forms of service, but the
same Lord"(1 Corinthians 12:4–5). Paul
means that the Spirit's presence is
shown in some way in each person for
the good all.

Some people are called to be leaders
of our Church. First, there are our
ordained ministers, our bishops,
priests, and deacons.

Besides ordained ministers, your school principal, the parish director of religious education, teachers, and catechists help the people of the parish know and live their faith. There may be other pastoral ministers in your parish too. Find out what each does.

The Church, especially through our parish, helps us to do God's will and to live for the kingdom of God. The Church also helps us to know the right thing to do and to have the courage to do it.

They serve by guiding the Church, helping us to worship God, and preaching the good news of Jesus.

The pope, the successor of Saint Peter, is the leader of the whole Catholic Church. He and the other bishops teach, govern, and sanctify the Church. The bishop is the leader of a diocese, and the pastor is the priest who is the leader of a parish.

Who are the leaders that guide and help us in the Church? What do they do?

Do you ever seek their help and guidance? Will you?

OUR CATHOLIC FAITH

O God, your greatness is seen throughout the whole world. We praise you.

Why do you think the Church gives us laws to live by?

The Laws of the Church

Today the Catholic Church is in countries all over the world. Catholic people speak many different languages and have many different customs. The Catholic Church is made up of hundreds of dioceses. Each diocese is made up of many parishes.

In each parish, Catholics join together to hear and preach the good news of Jesus, to pray, to celebrate the sacraments, to serve others, and to help build up the kingdom, or reign, of God. To help us do these things together, we follow the laws of the Church. These laws are shown and explained in the chart on the next page.
Study it carefully.

Complete the following activity using one of the Laws of the Church.

Keeping the law of the Church about

_____

_____

_____

can help me do God's loving will because

_____

_____

_____

I will try to obey this law better when I

_____

_____

_____

Take turns explaining the Laws of the Church in your own words.

Choose one law and tell how you will try to live it.

The Laws of the Church

1.	Celebrate Christ's resurrection every Sunday and on the holy days of obligation by taking part in the celebration of Mass and by avoiding unnecessary work.	This means taking special time each week to think about God's goodness to us. We think about the ways in which we are to put God first in our lives.
2.	Receive Holy Communion frequently and take part in the celebration of the sacrament of Reconciliation. At a minimum, Catholics are also to receive Holy Communion at least once between the First Sunday of Lent and Trinity Sunday. We must confess at least once a year if we have committed any serious, or mortal, sins.	By celebrating these sacraments frequently, we grow in our love for God. The Holy Spirit guides us in making good decisions in our daily lives.
3.	Study Catholic teachings throughout our lives and continue to grow in faith.	Learning about our faith helps us to live it more each day. We will also be better able to carry on Jesus' mission.
4.	Observe the marriage laws of the Catholic Church. Make sure children receive religious instruction and formation.	Children need love and guidance from parents and others who care for them. They also need to learn about and live their faith in a loving family.
5.	Strengthen and support the Church, including our parish, priests, the whole Church, and the pope.	We have a responsibility to support the work of the Church and carry on the mission of Jesus Christ.
6.	Do penance, including fasting and not eating meat on certain days.	When we do penance, we give thanks for God's goodness.
7.	Join in the missionary work of the Church.	Each of us is called to help missionary work by giving what money we can and by praying for our missionaries.

Our Catholic Faith

- Lord, we thank you for sharing your life and love with us.

- How does your parish community help you to carry on the mission of Jesus?

We Celebrate the Sacraments

As members of Jesus' Church, we come together in the Holy Spirit to worship God in the seven sacraments. The sacraments are seven powerful signs through which Jesus shares God's life and love with us.

Baptism, Confirmation, and Eucharist are called the sacraments of initiation. Through these sacraments we become and grow as members of the Church, the body of Christ. Through these sacraments the Holy Spirit helps us to do God's loving will and to live as disciples of Jesus Christ.

The sacraments of service are Matrimony and Holy Orders. Through these sacraments, some people are called to use the gifts and talents they have been given to serve the Church in special ways.

Our ordained ministers receive the sacrament of Holy Orders. In the sacrament of Matrimony, the Church blesses the special love married people have for each other.

In the sacraments of healing, the Church brings us God's healing and peace. These sacraments are the Anointing of the Sick and Reconciliation or Penance.

Taking part in the celebration of the sacraments with our parish community can help us to grow in our Catholic faith and to do God's will always. Through the sacraments, the Holy Spirit gives us the grace we need to live as Jesus' disciples. We join with others to give praise and honor to God. We worship God and give thanks for all his blessings.

Easter Duty

It is a law of the Church that we receive Holy Communion at least once a year between the First Sunday of Lent and Trinity Sunday. The Church made this law for a special reason.

A long time ago, some Catholics began to think that they should not receive Holy Communion frequently. They thought they were not worthy to receive our Lord Jesus Christ himself each week. They were forgetting why Jesus gave us the gift of himself in Holy Communion—to nourish us often and to strengthen us in living as his disciples.

That is why the Church wisely made the law to receive Holy Communion at least once during the seasons of Lent and Easter. The practice of receiving Communion during this time became known as "making our Easter duty."

We should not think of receiving Communion only as a duty, however. It is a great privilege and joy for us to receive Jesus. Even though we are never fully worthy of this great honor, Jesus wants us to receive him often in Holy Communion. He comes to us as our Bread of Life.

Use these words from the Mass to prepare yourself for Holy Communion:

Lord, I am not worthy to receive you,
   but only say the word and I shall
      be healed.

Learn by heart **Faith Summary**

- The Holy Spirit guides the whole Church in continuing Jesus' mission.

- Each baptized person has something special to do to carry on Jesus' mission.

- The laws of the Church help us to live as good Catholics.

Coming to Faith

Here are some things your parish church does to help you live for God's kingdom. Respond to each question.

- Your parish teaches you about God, Jesus, and the Holy Spirit through its religious education programs and the homilies at Mass.

Who helps you learn about your Catholic faith?

- Your parish invites members to volunteer for its various activities. The volunteers feed the hungry, take care of the lonely and the homeless, visit and pray with the sick, and reach out to people who are hurting.

How can you help care for others with your parish community?

- Your parish worships God and celebrates the seven sacraments.

How can you best take part in worshiping with your parish community?

How else does the Church help you live your Catholic faith?

Talk with your teacher about ways you and your family might use the "Faith Alive" section. Ask family members to work with you on doing the "I Believe" activity.

Practicing Faith

Create an IDEAGRAM you would like to send to the pope, your bishop, or your pastor to tell him how the Church can help and guide you better. Also tell how you will help him to do this.

Share your ideagrams. Then develop a group letter that you will send to our Holy Father at the Vatican in Rome.

IDEAGRAM   (Circle one)

pope   bishop   pastor

Here are some ways I think you can help me to live my Catholic faith:

_____

_____

Here are some ways I will try to help you:

_____

_____

REVIEW ▪ TEST

Circle the letter beside the correct answer.

1. Catholics must take part in Mass on

   a. each Sunday or Saturday evening.

   b. Independence Day.

   c. Thanksgiving Day.

   d. every first Friday.

2. Catholics must confess at least once a year if we have committed any

   a. mortal sin.

   b. venial sin.

   c. original sin.

   d. temptation.

3. Catholic parents must make sure their children receive

   a. religious instruction.

   b. a college education.

   c. Matrimony.

   d. Holy Orders.

4. All Catholics can join in the missionary work of the Church by

   a. going to the foreign missions.

   b. praying for our missionaries.

   c. supporting the United Nations.

   d. becoming priests.

5. How do you think the Laws of the Church help you?

   _____

   _____

FAITH ALIVE AT HOME AND IN THE PARISH

In this lesson your fourth grader has learned that young people, too, have a responsibility to carry on the mission of Jesus. One of the central teachings of the Second Vatican Council, echoing the earliest Christian communities, is that by Baptism all Christians are to participate actively in carrying on the mission of Jesus in the world.

In this chapter your child has also learned how the laws, or precepts, of the Church help us to live our faith. These laws help us to live a moral and prayerful life as we seek to build up the reign of God. You can find the Laws of the Church on page 215 of your child's text.

I Believe

Gather your family for an "I Believe" time. Have each person write or share one thing that he or she believes as a member of the Church. For example, "I believe that Jesus wants us to worship together at Mass each week." When all are finished, one person can write down what the family has shared and post it as "The Faith of Our Family."

Making a Family Plan

Gather as a family and decide on one thing you can all do together to help your parish. It can be something as simple as bringing up the gifts at Mass some Sunday.

Jesus, help us to be strong when we are tempted to do wrong.

OUR LIFE

Joan dragged her feet all the way home. She was thinking about what her father was going to ask her and how she was going to answer. If Joan told the truth about the place she had been, she would be grounded for a week! It would be so easy to make up a story about. . . .

Finish Joan's story. What choice will she make? Will it be a good one?

Mr. Fisher was a tough teacher and no one wanted to have him in class. Some students called him names behind his back and made up stories about him. Kirk felt uneasy about this, but he wanted to be part of the group. Would he have any friends if he refused to listen to the gossip?

Finish Kirk's story. What will he do?

When you have to make a hard choice, how do you decide what to do?

SHARING LIFE

Share your story endings. Then discuss: Have you ever been in situations like those of Joan or Kirk? Who helped you to make choices?

How do you know whether you have made good decisions?

Work in small groups.
Each group will receive a "letter" from someone asking advice about the way to solve a problem.

Discuss the problem together. Be sure to let your Christian faith guide you. Then prepare a written response. When all are ready, hand in your responses. Each one will be read aloud. The whole group will decide which response they think is best. Share together the reasons for your choice.

This week we will be learning more about the way Christians make good choices.

☀ We Will Learn

- Our conscience is a gift from God.

- We are guided by the teachings of the Catholic Church.

- We need to practice examining our conscience.

Our Catholic Faith

- Lord, we place our trust in you.
- How do you know whether something is right or wrong? What do you think about to help you decide?

Forming Our Conscience

Living for God's kingdom of justice and peace is not easy. We know that the Church helps us in many ways.

This year we have studied the Beatitudes and the Spiritual and Corporal Works of Mercy. We have learned the Ten Commandments, the Law of Love, and the Laws of the Church. We have been taught what God's loving will is for us.

We also have learned that the Holy Spirit helps us to make good choices and gives us the courage to do the right thing. But each of us must listen to our own heart when we make decisions. God has said, "I will place my law within them, and write it upon their hearts" (Jeremiah 31:33).

We need to follow our conscience. Our conscience is the ability we have to decide whether something is right or wrong. Our conscience is a gift from God. When our conscience is guided by the teachings of the Church, it helps us to know what is right and what is wrong.

Following our conscience means using what is in our mind and heart to make good decisions. Our thoughts and feelings are both important in helping us know what our conscience is telling us.

God the Holy Spirit speaks to us through our conscience. If we ask the Holy Spirit for help in making decisions, our prayers will be answered. The Holy Spirit also helps us to remember the teachings of Jesus and the Church.

We can pray to the Holy Spirit for the courage to do God's will, even though it may be hard for us at times. We form a good conscience by learning as much as we can about our Catholic faith and by praying often to the Holy Spirit for guidance.

Our parents or guardians and many other people in the Church can also help us to form a good conscience. We should ask them to help us when we have difficult decisions to make.

These people will tell us that it is not always easy to make the right choices.

But with the help of the Holy Spirit and other good Christians in our faith community, we can always do God's will and live for the kingdom of God.

You learned in chapter nine how to make a good choice. The more you practice making Christian choices this way, the easier it will be for you to develop and to follow your conscience.

List the steps in making a good Christian choice.

_____

_____

_____

_____

_____

What does it mean for you to follow your conscience?

How will you try to form a good Christian conscience?

OUR CATHOLIC FAITH

- Pray the Lord's Prayer together.
- Why do we need time to think about our love for God and our love for others?

Examining Our Conscience

To be good Christians we need to examine our consciences often. No matter how busy we are, we should try each day to think about our lives and the ways we are living as disciples of Jesus and members of the Church.

We need to take time to think about ways we love God and others. We ask ourselves whether we have sinned by doing things that we know are wrong or by not doing the good things we should do. Each time we do this, we are examining our conscience.

A very good time to examine our conscience is just before we fall asleep at night. We can ask the Holy Spirit to help us as we look back over our day. If we find that we have not always done God's will, we can ask him to forgive us. We can say an Act of Contrition. Or we can pray the Our Father, paying special attention to the words "forgive us our trespasses as we forgive those who trespass against us."

We usually begin our examination of conscience by asking ourselves how well we have followed the Law of Love. We think of the ways we have been living for God's kingdom of justice and peace.

Then we think about how well we have tried to live the Beatitudes, the Spiritual and Corporal Works of Mercy, and the Laws of the Church. We ask ourselves whether we have obeyed the Ten Commandments. We have studied all of these this year and can use them to help us to examine our conscience.

When we examine our conscience, we may ask ourselves questions like these.

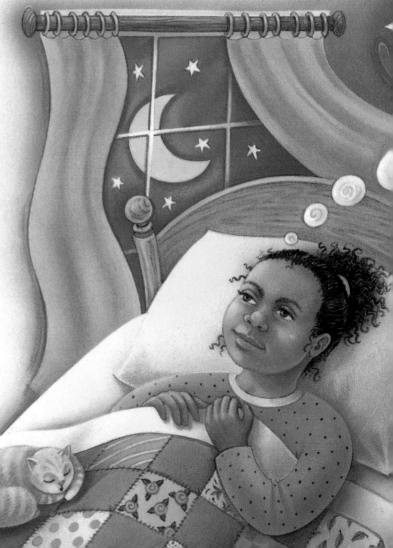

We make an **examination of conscience** when we ask ourselves, with the help of the Holy Spirit, how well we have obeyed God's law and have loved and served others.

EXAMINATION OF CONSCIENCE

How have I shown love for God?

- Does God come first in my life, or are other things more important to me?

- Have I used God's name with respect, or have I sometimes said God's name in anger?

- Have I remembered to pray to God?

- Do I go to Mass on Sundays or Saturday evenings and on holy days of obligation and take part in the celebration? Or have I missed Mass for no good reason?

How have I shown love for others?

- Have I cared as Jesus wants me to care for the poor, the hungry, and those who are mistreated or oppressed?

- Have I done my best to try to live for the kingdom of God?

- Have I obeyed and been respectful to the adults who are responsible for me?

- Do I share my things with others, or have I been selfish? Have I taken others' things without permission?

- Have I been truthful and fair, or have I lied and cheated?

How have I shown love for myself?

- Have I taken care of my body by eating properly, getting rest, and not doing anything that could harm me?

- Have I done anything to my body or another person's body that is disrespectful in thought, word, or action?

Why should you examine your conscience often?

What will you do today to show love for those most in need of love?

225

OUR CATHOLIC FAITH

▪ Holy Spirit, help me to know my sins and to be truly sorry for them.

▪ When is the best time for you to examine your conscience? Why?

The Sacrament of Reconciliation

Before taking part in the sacrament of Reconciliation, or Penance, we examine our conscience so that we will know what sins to confess. The priest will then be able to give us advice about ways to live better.

Reconciliation is a powerful sign through which Jesus forgives all our sins. Through this sacrament, we are reconciled, or united again, to God and to the community of the Church.

The sacrament of Reconciliation is a great prayer of praise and worship. In this sacrament we thank God for his love and forgiveness. We tell God we are sorry for our sins. We ask God's help to do his loving will and to avoid those things that tempt or lead us to sin.

The Sacred Heart of Jesus

The heart has always been a symbol of love. For Catholics, the heart of Jesus is a symbol of his great love for us. Because Jesus is both divine and human, he loves us as no one else can.

Each year soon after Pentecost, we celebrate the feast of the Sacred Heart of Jesus. Catholics do this to celebrate the love and forgiveness of God that comes to us in Jesus Christ our Savior.

Catholics often pray a litany in honor of the Sacred Heart of Jesus. A litany is a prayer in which we call repeatedly upon Jesus or Mary or the saints, using special titles or names. After each title or name, the community makes a response.

Here are two of the titles we use in the litany of the Sacred Heart. The response to each is "have mercy on us."

Heart of Jesus,
patient and full of mercy,
have mercy on us.

Heart of Jesus,
delight of all the saints,
have mercy on us.

At the end of the litany of the Sacred Heart, we pray together:

Jesus, gentle and humble of heart,
Touch our hearts and make
them like your own.

Try to find the complete litany of the Sacred Heart and pray it together.

Learn by heart **Faith Summary**

- Our conscience helps us to decide what is right or wrong.

- With the help of the Holy Spirit, we examine our conscience by asking ourselves how well we have lived God's law.

- We examine our conscience before celebrating the sacrament of Reconciliation.

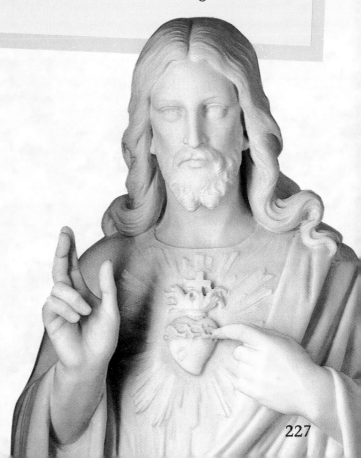

Coming To Faith

A great thinker once said, "The unexamined life is not worth living." What do you think he meant by that?

When do you examine your life, your conscience? When should you?

How does examining your conscience help you prepare for the sacrament of Reconciliation?

Practicing Faith

Take a few minutes to examine your conscience now. Use page 225 as a guide. Then gather together in a prayer circle.

Leader: Loving God, you call us to live as your people. Help us to follow your way of love.

All: Amen.

Reader 1: We will try to make good choices.

All: Help us to follow your way of love. (Make this response after each petition.)

Reader 2: We will be truthful. We will be honest. (**All:** Response)

Reader 3: We will be faithful. We will be obedient. (**All:** Response)

Reader 4: We will be fair. We will be peacemakers. (**All:** Response)

Leader: Let us pray the prayer Jesus taught us. Our Father. . . .

Talk with your teacher about ways you and your family might use the "Faith Alive" section. Pray "An Examination of Conscience Prayer" with your teacher and friends.

REVIEW ■ TEST

Circle the letter beside the correct answer.

1. We show love for God when we

    a. miss Mass often.

    b. say God's name in anger.

    c. pray only on Sundays.

    d. keep God first in our lives.

2. The ability to decide whether something is right or wrong is

    a. conscience.

    b. reconciliation.

    c. temptation.

    d. virtue.

3. In Reconciliation we confess to

    a. our parents.

    b. the teacher.

    c. the priest.

    d. our friends.

4. We celebrate God's love and forgiveness in

    a. conscience.

    b. Reconciliation.

    c. Matrimony.

    d. Holy Orders.

5. When should you examine your conscience? Why?

_____

_____

FAITH ALIVE ■ AT HOME AND IN THE PARISH

In this chapter, your fourth grader has learned how, why, and when to examine his or her conscience. Have your child show you the questions used as an examination of conscience.

As an adult, it may be helpful for you to reflect on difficult choices you have had to make and the process you used when making these choices. Consider how and how often you examine your own conscience—not necessarily to highlight weaknesses but more to challenge yourself to greater vitality and fidelity in living your Christian faith.

† An Examination of Conscience Prayer

Holy Spirit, fill me with your wisdom so I will see what I have to change. Fill me with your courage, so I will change it.

Celebrating Reconciliation

In the Communal Rite of Reconciliation, we gather as a community to celebrate God's forgiveness of us and to forgive one another. As a family, try to attend the next communal rite held in your parish. Afterwards, share with one another how you felt about the celebration.

25 We Celebrate Reconciliation

Dear God, help us to be forgiving and compassionate people.

Our Life

There once was a poor slave in Rome whose name was Androcles. He ran away from his cruel master and hid in a cave. Soon he fell asleep. A great noise suddenly woke him. A huge lion had come roaring into the cave. Androcles was terrified, but soon he noticed that the lion was limping badly. There was a large thorn in his paw. Androcles felt sorry for the lion. He picked up his paw. The lion leaned his head on Androcles' shoulder as if he knew Androcles would help him. Androcles pulled the thorn out quickly and the lion was so happy he jumped around like a puppy. That night the two slept side by side like two friends.

Eventually Androcles was captured. As a runaway slave, he was condemned to face the lions in the arena. He was led forth trembling, his eyes closed. The hungry lion rushed at him and to everyone's surprise, he lay down at Androcles' feet and rubbed his head against him. It was his old friend. The people were astonished. "Androcles and the lion must be set free!" they shouted. Many felt that the slave and the lion had taught them all how to live.

What is the lesson that Androcles and the lion taught?

Sharing Life

Talk together about things that can separate people from one another.

How can we be reconciled with one another? with God?

Work with a partner. Look through a newspaper and circle any story you find that shows how people are separated one from another. Decide together what could be done to bring about reconciliation.

Share all the reconciliation ideas from the group. Then design a poster that speaks about the need for reconciliation in our world. Choose a title for your poster and display it in your school.

This week we will learn more about the importance of being reconcilers and about the sacrament of Reconciliation.

We Will Learn

- We celebrate God's mercy and forgiveness in the sacrament of Reconciliation.

- We can take part in the Individual Rite and the Communal Rite of Reconciliation.

- Jesus asks us to be reconcilers in our family, neighborhood, school, and world.

■ God of mercy, help me to show Your mercy to others.

■ Is it easy to forgive others? Explain.

Forgiving and Being Forgiven

Jesus died to save us from our sins and to reconcile us with God and one another. Jesus wants us never to be separated from God by serious sin.

All of us need to forgive and be forgiven. There are many times when we need to be reconciled, or united again, with people who hurt us. We need to forgive them. Jesus wants us to forgive others.

One time Peter asked, "Lord, if my brother sins against me, how often must I forgive him? As many as seven times?"

Jesus answered, "I say to you, not seven times but seventy-seven times."
Matthew 18:21–22

That was Jesus' way of saying that we must *always* forgive others.

By the sacrament of Baptism, each of us is set free from original sin. We share in God's own life as his children. But we still need God's help to overcome sin in our world.

Jesus knew that sometimes we would sin. We would need God's forgiveness for the sins committed after Baptism.

Jesus gave his disciples the power to forgive sins in God's name. Jesus said to them: "Whose sins you forgive are forgiven them, and whose sins you retain are retained."
John 20:23

When we have sinned, God is always ready to forgive us. When we are sorry, we celebrate God's forgiveness in the sacrament of Reconciliation, or Penance.

The power to forgive sins in God's name has been passed on in our Church. In the sacrament of Reconciliation, our bishops and priests act in the name of God and of the Christian community to forgive our sins.

There are two ways we can take part in the celebration of the sacrament of Reconciliation: by ourselves with the priest (Individual Rite), or with others and the priest (Communal Rite).

THE INDIVIDUAL RITE

Absolution is the prayer the priest says asking forgiveness of our sins.

① You make the sign of the cross with the priest. You may kneel behind a screen or sit and talk face-to-face with the priest.

② The priest or you may read a story from the Bible about God's love and forgiveness.

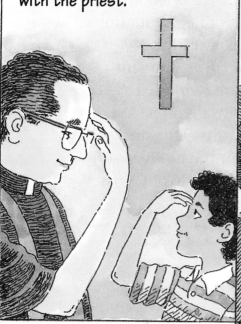

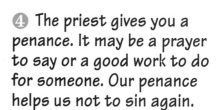

③ You confess your sins to God by telling them to the priest. The priest talks to you to help you see how you can avoid sinning in the future.

④ The priest gives you a penance. It may be a prayer to say or a good work to do for someone. Our penance helps us not to sin again.

⑤ The priest asks you to pray an Act of Contrition to tell God that you are sorry and will try to sin no more.

⑦ With the priest, you thank God for God's mercy and forgiveness.

⑥ In the name of God and the whole Christian community, the priest absolves you from your sins. He extends his hand over your head as he prays the words of absolution.

What happens in the Individual Rite of Reconciliation?

How often does our faith tell us to forgive others? Will you try?

233

OUR CATHOLIC FAITH

- Pray an Act of Contrition together.

- Why do you think the sacrament of Reconciliation is so important for us?

Reconciliation

Some Catholics do not take part in the sacrament of Reconciliation because they are afraid or ashamed to tell the priest what they have done. Others think that their sin is too big for God to forgive. But God is always ready to forgive us when we are sorry.

During the celebration of Reconciliation, we may tell the priest our hurts and worries. The priest will give us good advice and will try to help us. He will not tell anyone what we say, so we should not be afraid to talk to him about anything.

Jesus taught us the importance of always being ready to forgive and be forgiven. He said, that if you are about to offer your gift to God at the altar and you remember that someone has something against you, you must leave your gift in front of the altar, go at once and make peace with this person, and only then come back and offer your gift to God.

Based on Matthew 5:23–24

Sometimes our parish community gathers together to celebrate the sacrament of Reconciliation. When we take part in the celebration of this sacrament together, we are reminded that our sins always affect the whole community. Our sins take away from the holiness of the Church, the body of Christ.

THE COMMUNAL RITE

This is how we take part in the Communal Rite with the priest and our parish community.

- We sing an opening hymn and the priest greets us. The priest prays an opening prayer.

- We listen to a reading from the Bible and a homily.

- We examine our conscience.

- We say an Act of Contrition together.

- We may pray a litany or sing a song, and then pray the Our Father.

- We confess our sins to a priest in private. In the name of God and the Christian community, the priest gives us a penance and absolution.

- We pray as we conclude our celebration. The priest blesses us, and we go in the peace and joy of Christ.

Write a prayer that you might pray to the Holy Spirit to help you prepare for the celebration of Reconciliation.

† _____

_____

_____

_____

How do we celebrate the Communal Rite of Reconciliation?

When do you think you might celebrate the sacrament of Reconciliation?

OUR CATHOLIC FAITH

Loving God, help us to be reconcilers, and peacemakers.

What advice would you give to someone who never takes part in the sacrament of Reconciliation?

We Are Reconcilers

The sacrament of Reconciliation helps us to build up God's kingdom of justice and peace. Through this sacrament, Jesus asks each of us to be reconcilers and peacemakers.

We can be reconcilers when we help others understand what Saint Paul told the first Christians that God does not keep a record of our sins. God has given us the message through Christ that God wants everyone to be his friends.

After celebrating the sacrament of Reconciliation, we should promise God that we will be reconcilers and peacemakers in our daily lives. We are reconcilers when we try to do God's loving will and bring his peace to others. We can help others who may be fighting, hurt, or angry. We can be reconcilers in our home, in our school, and in our neighborhood. We can pray and work for justice and peace in our world.

We are reconcilers when we forgive others who have hurt or sinned against us. We forgive others because we, too, need God's forgiveness.

We are reconcilers when we help people in our school or parish who feel "left out." Some people want to hurt others who are different from them. They do not want to be friends with anyone who is not the same as they are. We can ask the Holy Spirit to help us to stop such prejudice.

We are reconcilers when we talk to our families, our teachers, and our parish leaders about what we can do to build the kingdom, or reign, of God.

Confessing Our Sins

When Catholics go to confession, they usually celebrate the sacrament either in a reconciliation room or a confessional box. These are the usual places for the celebration of the sacrament. But do you know that a priest can hear confessions at any time and in any place?

When Catholics are sick and unable to go to the church, the priest will go to them. He can hear their confession in their homes or at the hospital. A priest is always happy to visit the sick and celebrate the sacrament of Reconciliation, as well as the sacrament of Anointing of the Sick with them.

Whether he is at home or traveling, a priest may be called upon to hear confessions in an emergency. For example, a priest may give absolution at the scene of an accident. Some priests who work as military chaplains even celebrate this sacrament on battlefields or aboard warships.

The Church wants the grace of the sacrament of Reconciliation to be available to us at all times. All of us are called to a deep appreciation of this sacrament and to celebrate it regularly.

Learn by heart **Faith Summary**

- We celebrate God's mercy and forgiveness in the sacrament of Reconciliation.

- We can take part in the sacrament of Reconciliation alone with the priest or with the community and the priest.

- Jesus asks us to be reconcilers in our family, neighborhood, school, and world.

COMING TO FAITH

When should people take part in the sacrament of Reconciliation? Why?

To take part in the sacrament of Reconciliation:

1. Examine your _____.

2. Tell your _____ to God through the priest.

3. Accept the _____ the priest gives you.

4. Be sorry and say an Act of

   _____.

5. Receive _____ from the priest.

6. Remember to do your _____ and not to sin again.

PRACTICING FAITH

Plan with your group a parish flyer to be given out or a banner to be displayed in your church. Discuss the design and what the message will say to remind everyone of Reconciliation.

Talk with your teacher about ways you and your family might use the "Faith Alive" section. Ask a family member to help you learn the Act of Contrition by heart. Then pray the Act of Contrition with your teacher and friends.

REVIEW ▪ TEST

Read through the list of actions and cross out any that are not part of the Individual Rite of Reconciliation. Then put the actions in the correct order by numbering them 1 to 5.

_____ The priest absolves us.

_____ The priest gives us a penance.

_____ We confess our sins.

_____ We are blessed with holy water.

_____ The priest welcomes us, and we make the sign of the cross.

_____ We pray an Act of Contrition.

When will you celebrate the sacrament of Reconciliation?

_____

_____

FAITH ALIVE AT HOME AND IN THE PARISH

Your fourth grader has reviewed the Individual Rite and the Communal Rite of the sacrament of Reconciliation. Talk to your child about what happens in the celebration of this sacrament. Share your own appreciation for it and what it means for you to experience the mercy and love of God in this wonderful sacrament. Make sure he or she can pray an Act of Contrition from memory.

Act of Contrition
My God,
I am sorry for my sins with all my heart.
In choosing to do wrong
and failing to do good,
I have sinned against you
whom I should love above all things.

I firmly intend, with your help,
to do penance,
to sin no more,
and to avoid whatever leads me to sin.
Our Savior Jesus Christ
suffered and died for us.
In his name, my God, have mercy.

Saying "I'm Sorry"

Asking forgiveness is a very difficult thing for most of us to do. It can be especially difficult for a child. Plan ways to make it easier for your child to express sorrow. Discuss with him or her ways to do this, for example, at bedtime prayer, with a hug, or a flower, and a promise to do better. Do not hesitate yourself to say "I'm sorry" to or in front of your child.

26 We Celebrate the Eucharist

Jesus, help us to recognize you in all the many ways you are present in our lives.

Our Life

On the first Easter Sunday after Jesus had risen from the dead, two of his disciples were walking from Jerusalem to the village of Emmaus. On the way they met a man who began to walk with them. It was Jesus, but they did not recognize him.

The stranger began to explain the Scriptures to the two disciples. He showed how everything that had happened to him had been spoken of in the Old Testament. When they got close to Emmaus, the men begged Jesus to stay and eat with them.

When they sat down to eat, Jesus broke the bread and gave it to them. Immediately they recognized him in the breaking of the bread. Then Jesus disappeared from their sight.

The two disciples hurried back to Jerusalem to tell the others that Jesus had risen. They had come to know Jesus in the breaking of the bread.
Based on Luke 24:13–35

How did the two disciples of Jesus recognize him?

Do you feel close to Jesus when you receive him in Holy Communion?

What do you usually say to him?

Sharing Life

Why do you think the two disciples did not recognize Jesus at first?

Together with your group make a list of times when we might not recognize Jesus among us.

Discuss why we might miss Him.

240

Listen carefully as the story of the Last Supper is read (Luke 22:14–20). Then read again quietly the story of Jesus meeting with the disciples on the way to Emmaus (page 240).

Now work in small groups. Some groups will plan and dramatize the story of the Last Supper. Other groups will plan and dramatize the story of Emmaus.

Present your dramatizations. Then discuss together what might have caused the disciples finally to recognize Jesus "in the breaking of the bread."

This week we will be discovering more about what it means for us to recognize Jesus in the Eucharist.

We Will Learn

- We listen to God's word during the Liturgy of the Word.

- At Mass, the bread and wine become the Body and Blood of Christ.

- We must plan how we will live for the kingdom, or reign, of God.

May all people praise you, O God.

Do you ever feel like not taking part in the Mass? Why is this so? What can help?

1. sign of cross
2. priest welcomes us

The Introductory Rites

As a worshiping assembly, we also recognize the risen Christ in the breaking of the bread. This is the Mass, and we begin the Mass with the sign of the cross. Our priest celebrant welcomes us and reminds us that the Holy Spirit is with us.

3. The priest then leads us in asking for God's mercy and forgiveness. We praise God by praying *4* "Glory to God in the highest." *5* Then the priest gathers up our prayers and prays to God in our name.

Liturgy of the Word

6. Now we listen carefully as God speaks to us through the different readings from the Bible.

The first reading is usually from the Old Testament. We hear about God's love and mercy for the people who lived long before Jesus was born. God wants us to learn and live the lessons of courage, patience, forgiveness, justice, and love that he taught the people of Israel.

7. Then we sing or say a psalm. The psalms are songs of thanksgiving, praise, sorrow, and petition to God.

8. Next we listen to letters, or epistles, written by Jesus' first disciples. They tell us that Jesus calls each of us to do God's loving will and to work to bring about his kingdom of justice and peace.

9. We stand to hear the gospel. The word *gospel* means "good news." In the gospel, Jesus speaks to us today, as he did to his friends long ago. He tells us that we are to try to love one another as he loves us.

10. After reading the gospel, the priest or deacon explains the meaning of the Scriptures to us in a homily. Then we

11. stand and pray the creed, a summary of our beliefs. We say that we believe in God and in all that the Church teaches us.

12. Then we say the Prayer of the Faithful. We pray for our Church and its leaders, for those who lead our country, and for the needs of our family, friends, and parish community. We pray for those who suffer and for people everywhere.

FAITH WORD

Liturgy means the official public worship of the Church.

Now that we have heard the word of God and spoken aloud our prayers as a worshiping assembly, we are ready to celebrate the Liturgy of the Eucharist.

- Explain what happens during the Introductory Rites of the Mass.

- How can you listen more carefully to the readings at Mass?

OUR CATHOLIC FAITH

■ Your word, O God, is a lamp to guide me and a light for my path.

■ What is the best gift we can offer God at Mass?

The Liturgy of the Eucharist

After the Liturgy of the Word, we are ready for the Liturgy of the Eucharist. *Eucharist* means "thanksgiving." During this part of the Mass, we thank God for all his blessings and for giving us Jesus, our Savior.

We begin the Liturgy of the Eucharist by bringing gifts of bread and wine to the altar. The bread and wine are gifts grown from the earth. They stand for us and all we have.

After our gifts have been brought to the altar, the priest begins the Eucharistic Prayer. The priest leads the entire assembly in the Eucharistic Prayer by asking the Holy Spirit to come upon our gifts to make them holy. The priest says and does what Jesus said and did at the Last Supper. The priest says over the bread, "This is my body." He says over the cup of wine, "This is the cup of my blood."

Through the power of the Holy Spirit and the words and actions of the priest, the bread and wine become the Body and Blood of Christ. This part of the Mass is called the consecration. After this, we proclaim the mystery of faith.

During the Eucharistic Prayer, we offer to God the Father all that we have and all that we are. The Eucharistic Prayer ends with a prayer of praise. The priest says of Jesus,
"Through him,
with him,
in him,
in the unity of the Holy Spirit,
all glory and honor is yours,
almighty Father,
for ever and ever."
We answer, "Amen."

Next comes the Communion of the Mass. We pray together <u>the Our Father</u> 17. as Jesus taught us. We ask for God's forgiveness and promise to forgive those whom we have offended. We share a sign of peace with one another to show we are trying to bring about the peace of God's kingdom.

19. This is followed by the breaking of the Bread, reminding us that we all share in the one Body of Christ.

20. Now we can receive Jesus Christ in Holy Communion. To show respect for Jesus, our Bread of Life, we keep the eucharistic fast. This means that we do not eat or drink anything—except water or medicine if necessary—for one hour before Communion.

21. After Holy Communion, we have quiet time to thank Jesus for giving us the gift of himself. We ask him to help us live as his disciples. Each time we receive Jesus in Holy Communion, we are strengthened to do God's loving will and live for his kingdom of justice and peace.

Complete this prayer. Pray it after receiving Holy Communion.

† Jesus, I believe you are with me and really present in the Eucharist. Thank you for loving me so much. Please help me live each day as your disciple and friend. Please help me live for God's kingdom by

_____

_____

_____

_____

_____

■ What happens during the Liturgy of the Eucharist?

■ What will you say to Jesus the next time you receive Holy Communion?

OUR CATHOLIC FAITH

- Glory to the Father, and to the Son, and to the Holy Spirit.

- Will you be able to take part more fully in the Mass now? Why or why not?

Concluding Rite

As the Mass ends, the priest blesses us all in God's name. We make the sign of the cross and answer, "Amen."

The priest reminds us to live for God's kingdom of justice and peace. We hear him or the deacon say, "Go in peace to love and serve the Lord."

We answer, "Thanks be to God." We leave Mass prepared to continue living for the kingdom, or reign, of God. As Catholics, we know that celebrating the Mass is the most important thing we do together. It is in the Mass that we are strengthened to do what God wants.

God wants us to choose to follow the Law of Love and the Ten Commandments and to live the Beatitudes and the Corporal and Spiritual Works of Mercy.

God the Father gave us Jesus, the Son of God, and the Holy Spirit to help us. Each time we celebrate the Eucharist, we will grow as the people of God. It is up to us to choose to live as disciples of Jesus Christ.

Mass in a prison chapel

GO IN PEACE

The Feast of Corpus Christi

Each year on the second Sunday after Pentecost, the Church celebrates the feast of the Body and Blood of Christ. Catholics also call this day the feast of Corpus Christi. The words *Corpus Christi* are Latin for "the Body of Christ."

Corpus Christi is a wonderful day on which Catholics all around the world remember and celebrate the real presence of Christ in the Eucharist. On this day, we take the time to show special love and reverence for the Eucharist, our Bread of Life.

Very often a parish community will have a procession with the Blessed Sacrament. The whole parish gathers behind the priest or deacon, who carries the Blessed Sacrament in a special container in which the Host can be seen. The container is called the *monstrance*. If the weather is good, the procession might even go outside the church to the surrounding neighborhood.

In some countries, everyone joins in the procession, especially in small towns and villages. Sometimes the procession will start at the parish church, move through the very center of the town, and return to the Church again.

Invite your family or friends to make a visit with you to the Blessed Sacrament this week. Spend a few moments in prayer with Jesus.

Learn by heart   Faith Summary

- The Mass is made up of the Liturgy of the Word and the Liturgy of the Eucharist.

- We listen to readings from the Bible during the Liturgy of the Word.

- During the Liturgy of the Eucharist the bread and wine become the Body and Blood of Christ.

COMING TO FAITH

What have you learned that will help you to take part in the Mass more fully?

Complete this prayer to be said after Holy Communion.

✝ Jesus, I believe you are with me. Thank you for loving me so much. Please help me live each day as your friend by. . . .

PRACTICING FAITH

Write a note to Jesus telling him how you will try to be his faithful disciple during vacation. Seal your note and hold it in your hand as you join your friends in a prayer circle.

Leader: Our time together is coming to an end. Let us give thanks to Jesus for all the gifts and graces we have been given this past year.

Person 1: Jesus, we bring a flower as a sign of our growing together with you.

Person 2: Jesus, we bring our *Coming to God's Love* book as a sign that we have grown as your disciples.

Person 3: Jesus, we bring you our notes as a sign of our love and our desire to stay close to you always.

Go around the circle. Each one in turn can express thanks for Jesus, for catechists, friends, parents, parish, and others. Begin by saying, "We thank you for. . . ."

Then sing together:

Now thank we all our God,
With hearts, and hands, and voices,
Who wondrous things has done,
In whom his world rejoices;
Who from our mother's arms
Has blessed us on our way
With countless gifts of love,
And still is ours today.

Conclude by sharing a sign of peace.

Talk with your teacher about ways you and your family might use the "Faith Alive" section. You might want especially to share your summer calendar with your family.

248

REVIEW ■ TEST

Fill in the blanks to complete the statements.

1. We begin the Liturgy of the _____ by bringing gifts of bread and wine to the altar.

2. The word _____ means "good news."

3. In the Liturgy of the _____ we listen to readings from the Bible.

4. In _____ we receive Jesus himself.

5. How will you try to take a more active part in the Mass this week?

_____

_____

FAITH ALIVE AT HOME AND IN THE PARISH

This year your fourth grader has learned to come to God's love through the practice of the Law of Love, the Beatitudes, the Corporal and Spiritual Works of Mercy, the Ten Commandments, and the Laws of the Church, as well as by prayer, celebration of the sacraments, and service to others. We have surveyed much of the horizon of Christian living in our Catholic morality and spirituality.

What a wonderful gift our faith is! But it is a gift that needs to be nurtured 365 days a year. Ask God to help you model for your child a faith life that is rich and open to growth at all times. Always rely on the community of the Church for guidance and support.

A Summer Calendar

Help your child create a large calendar for the summer months. Encourage him or her to mark with a special sign or drawing important times to think about and to do things out of love for God. Mark each weekend Mass, for example, as well as August 15, a holy day of obligation. Also mark times when your child chooses to do something special for another person.

Our Life

When the Nazi army invaded Poland in 1939, one of the first people they tried to silence was Father Maximilian Kolbe. Because of his courageous writing and preaching against the invaders, he was arrested and sent to Auschwitz, one of the worst of the Nazi concentration camps.

One July morning in 1941, the camp commander lined up all the prisoners. He told them that a man had escaped the night before. As a result, he selected ten people to be put in a dark bunker and left to die of starvation. One of the men began to plead with the commandant, "My wife, my poor children!" he cried.

Suddenly, Father Kolbe stepped forward. "Let me take the place of that man," he said.

During the terrible weeks that followed, those outside did not hear the usual screams and cries of despair. They heard the faint sounds of singing. When the bunker door opened on August 14, Father Kolbe was alive. He was still smiling when they killed him.

On August 14, 1982, Pope John Paul II named Maximilian Kolbe a saint of the Church.

Tell in your own words why you think Father Kolbe is a saint.

Sharing Life

Talk together about what the lives of the saints can teach us. How do you think they can help us?

Make a list of the qualities that you think a saint would have.

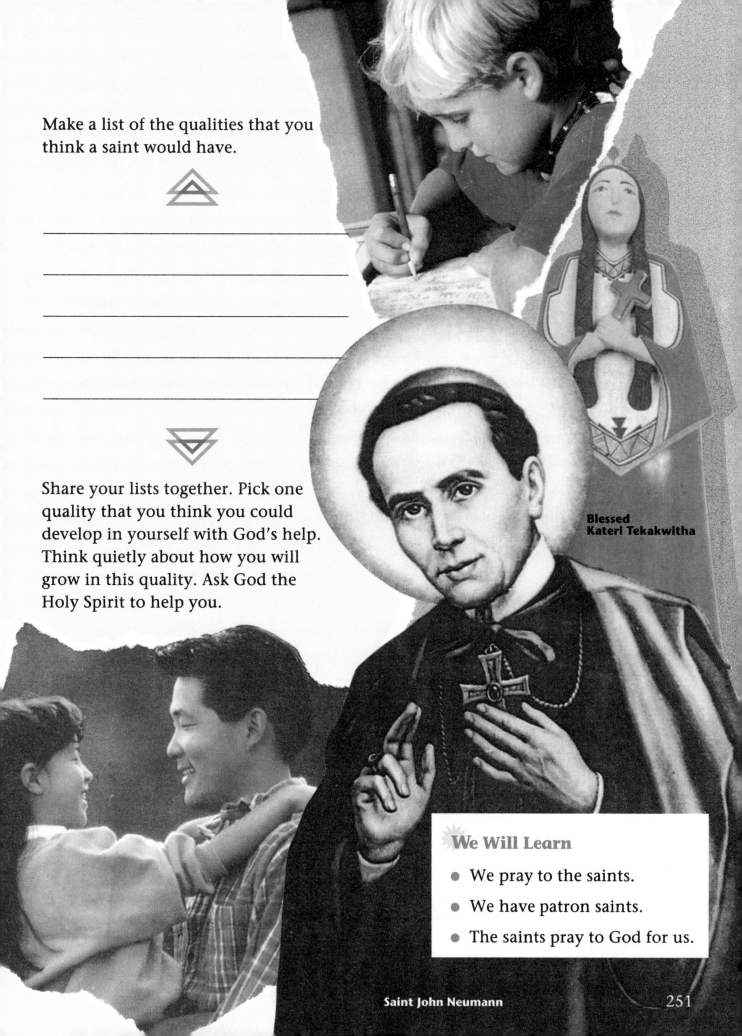

_____

_____

_____

_____

_____

Share your lists together. Pick one quality that you think you could develop in yourself with God's help. Think quietly about how you will grow in this quality. Ask God the Holy Spirit to help you.

Blessed Kateri Tekakwitha

We Will Learn

- We pray to the saints.
- We have patron saints.
- The saints pray to God for us.

Saint John Neumann

Catholics believe that those who have died and who are in God's presence are still united with us. This is why we pray to the saints and ask them to help us.

Saints are women and men who have tried their best to do God's will and to be disciples of Jesus Christ. The saints are people like us who led holy lives.

The Church honors these men and women by canonizing, or naming, them saints. The Church tells us that they are with God in heaven.

A special day is sometimes set aside for remembering a saint each year. This day is called the saint's feast day.

By remembering the example of the saints, we learn ways to live our faith. By praying to them, we receive help to do God's will.

Patron Saints

Catholics often choose the names of saints for their children. We call these saints our patron saints. The Church also names saints to be patron saints of places or activities. For example, Saint Cecilia is the patron saint of musicians.

The patron saint of the United States is Mary, the mother of Jesus. We honor and pray to Mary under her title of the Immaculate Conception on December 8.

The patron saint of Mexico is Mary, Our Lady of Guadalupe (feast day, December 12). The people of Mexico remember and celebrate that Mary appeared to Juan Diego. Blessed Juan Diego was a poor Aztec Indian in Mexico. Mary asked him to have a church built in her honor at Guadalupe.

The patron saint of South America is Saint Rose of Lima (August 23). Her full name was Isabel de Santa Maria de Flores. She took the name Rose at Confirmation and lived in Lima, Peru, where she cared for the sick. Even while she was still living, many people asked for her prayers.

St. Cecilia

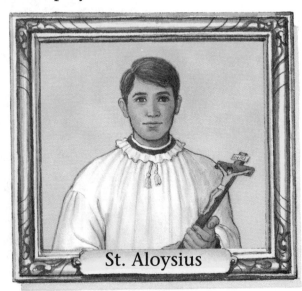

St. Aloysius

Does your parish have a patron saint? Write his or her name here:

_____

Some people pray to saints to ask them for help in their work. Saint Joseph, the foster father of Jesus, is honored on May 1 as the patron saint of workers.

Sometimes we pray to special saints for help in our studies. The patron saint of schools is Saint Thomas Aquinas (January 28).

Saint Aloysius Gonzaga is the patron saint of young people (June 21). Saint Aloysius was born in Italy. He taught religion to poor people and died at a very young age.

St. Frances Cabrini

Nurses pray to Saint Camillus (July 14). Saint Camillus ran a hospital in Rome. He became a priest and cared for the sick with special love.

Saint Frances Cabrini is the patron saint of people who leave home to go to a new land (November 13).

Saints were people just like us. They did the kinds of things that we do, too. There are women, men, and children who are living saints today. They follow the way of Jesus. They bring God's love to all people.

COMING TO FAITH

Explain why we honor the saints.

Can you be a saint? How?

Draw or paste a picture of your patron or favorite saint here. Write something about this saint.

PRACTICING FAITH
A Prayer Service for Saints

Opening Song

Sing to the tune of "When the Saints Go Marching In."

Oh celebrate
With all God's saints.
They tried to do God's loving will.
They are the followers of Jesus,
Shining brightly in God's love.

Leader: We come together to celebrate the saints. Let us begin by praying to our patron saints.

All: (Each student names his or her patron saint. The other students say, Saint _____ , pray for us.)

Leader: Let us pray to the saints we have learned about this week. The response is "Pray for us."

Immaculate Mary, Mother of God, patron saint of the United States, ...

Our Lady of Guadalupe, patron saint of Mexico, ...

Saint Rose of Lima, patron saint of South America, ...

Saint Joseph, patron saint of workers, ...

Saint Thomas Aquinas, patron saint of schools, ...

Saint Aloysius Gonzaga, patron saint of young people, ...

Saint Camillus, patron saint of nurses, ...

Saint Frances Cabrini, patron saint of immigrants, ...

All you saints of God, ...

Leader: Let us honor the patron saint or special saint of our parish.

Reader: (One member of the group reads a report of the parish's patron or special saint.)

All: (Each person carries a picture or symbol of her or his patron saint to the front of the room and either places it on a table or hangs it on the bulletin board.)

Closing Hymn

Sing to the tune of "Holy, Holy, Holy."

Alle-Alle-luia
Celebrate the saints.
They follow Jesus and
Show us all God's love.
Alle-Alle-luia
All God's holy people
Help us to live our faith
And do God's loving will.

Talk with your teacher about ways you and your family might use the "Faith Alive" section. Share one of the songs you learned about the saints.

REVIEW ▪ TEST

Match.

1. Saint Aloysius Gonzaga ⎯⎯ ran a hospital in Rome

2. Saint Frances Cabrini ⎯⎯ patron saint of immigrants

3. Saint Camillus ⎯⎯ patron saint of the United States

4. Saint Rose of Lima ⎯⎯ patron saint of young people

⎯⎯ cared for the sick in Peru

5. Can you begin now to be a saint? How?

_____

_____

FAITH ALIVE AT HOME AND IN THE PARISH

In this chapter your fourth grader was introduced to several saints of the Church. He or she learned that these people were canonized as saints because they modeled their lives on Jesus Christ.

Fourth graders have a natural interest in these heroines and heroes of the Church. Remind your child that the saints were ordinary people who simply tried to give their best to God everyday and to live as disciples of Jesus. Help your child discover the unique gifts he or she has to offer to God and others.

Learn by heart **Faith Summary**

● Saints are people who tried their best to do God's loving will.

● By remembering the saints and asking their help we learn to live our faith and to do God's will.

Mary, Queen
of the rosary,
pray for us.

Our Life

One of the most beautiful and important gifts God has given us is memory. Imagine what it would be like to have no memory of our past. It does not matter whether our memories are happy or sad—we would be lost without them.

Take a minute now to name a happy memory you have. Then name a sad memory. If you can think of the most wonderful memory of all that you have, name that, too.

Sharing Life

Share some of your memories with your friends.

Sometimes we cannot remember people, but only stories about them. What do you remember about Jesus and Mary? Why are those memories important to you?

Draw or write a story or a poem about one of your favorite stories of Jesus or Mary. Share your story. Explain what you learn from it for your own life.

Detail of *The Nativity,* **Guido Reni, 1600s**
Detail of *The Last Supper,* **Titian, 1500s**

This week we will learn a special way that Catholics remember Jesus and Mary.

We Will Learn

- The rosary is a special prayer for Catholics.

- The rosary helps us to remember Jesus and Mary.

- There are joyful, sorrowful, and glorious mysteries of the rosary.

We Pray the Rosary

One of the prayers we say to the Blessed Virgin Mary is the rosary. The rosary helps us to remember the lives of Jesus and Mary. We begin the rosary by praying the Apostles' Creed on the cross of the rosary.

On the large bead and three smaller beads that follow, we pray one Our Father and three Hail Marys. This is followed by one Glory to the Father.

Then we pray the five decades, or five groups of ten beads. On the one large bead before each decade, we pray an Our Father. On each of the ten smaller beads, we pray a Hail Mary. At the end of each decade, we pray the Glory to the Father. The entire rosary concludes with the Hail, Holy Queen prayer.

Annunciation, **Dante Gabriel Rossetti, 1849**

Mysteries of the Rosary

While we are praying the rosary, we think of events that took place in the lives of Jesus and Mary. We call these the mysteries of the rosary.

In the joyful mysteries, we think about the happy events in the lives of Jesus and Mary.

The Joyful Mysteries
- the annunciation
- the visitation
- the birth of Jesus
- the presentation of Jesus in the Temple
- the finding of Jesus in the Temple

Sometimes we think of the sorrowful events in the lives of Jesus and Mary.

The Sorrowful Mysteries
- the agony in the garden
- the scourging at the pillar
- the crowning with thorns
- the carrying of the cross
- the crucifixion and death of Jesus

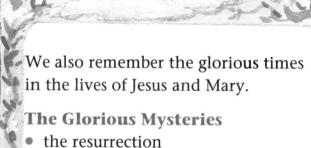

We also remember the glorious times in the lives of Jesus and Mary.

The Glorious Mysteries
- the resurrection
- the ascension
- the descent of the Holy Spirit upon the disciples
- the assumption of Mary into heaven
- the coronation of Mary as queen of heaven

COMING TO FAITH

With a partner, take turns explaining how we pray the rosary.

What do the mysteries of the rosary help us to remember?

May is the month of our Blessed Mother. During this month Catholics honor Mary in many different ways. How can you show your love for Mary in a special way during May?

PRACTICING FAITH
A May Crowning

Opening Hymn

"Hail Mary"

Leader: Through the angel Gabriel, God asked Mary to be the mother of his Son. Mary said: "I am the Lord's servant. May it happen to me as you have said."

All: Holy Mary, pray for us.

Leader: Let us pray a litany to Mary. The response is "Pray for us."
Holy Mother of God,. . .
Mother of Christ,. . .
Mother of the Church,. . .

Leader: When Jesus was born in Bethlehem, shepherds came from the hills. They told Mary and Joseph about the army of angels who had appeared to them and had told them about this Child. "Mary remembered all these things and thought deeply about them."

Sinless Mother,. . .
Mother of good counsel,. . .
Mother of our Savior,. . .

Leader: When Jesus was dying on the cross, he saw his Mother and his friend John standing there. He said to John: "She is your mother."

Health of the sick,. . .
Comfort of the troubled,. . .
Help of Christians,. . .

Leader: Let us all gather around the statue of Mary. These flowers are a symbol of our love.

Crowning Ceremony

As everyone sings the closing hymn, one member of your group places a crown of flowers on the statue of Mary.

Closing Hymn

Immaculate Mary, your praises
  we sing.
You reign now in heaven with
  Jesus our King.
Ave, ave, ave Maria!
Ave, ave, ave Maria!

Talk with your teacher about ways you and your family might use the "Faith Alive" section. You might pray a decade of the rosary together. Tell your family about the May Crowning you have shared with your friends.

REVIEW ▪ TEST

Answer.

1. Name a joyful mystery of the rosary.

_____

2. Name a sorrowful mystery of the rosary.

_____

3. Name a glorious mystery of the rosary.

_____

4. What prayer do we say on the large bead between each decade?

_____

5. What prayer do you like to pray to Mary? Explain.

_____

_____

FAITH ALIVE AT HOME AND IN THE PARISH

In this chapter your fourth grader was introduced in a formal way to the rosary, an ancient Catholic devotion to Mary, the Mother of God. It is important that your child understand and appreciate this devotion as a part of our Catholic heritage. The rosary is not simply a repetition of prayers but a meditation experience on the joyful, sorrowful, and glorious mysteries—special events in the lives of Jesus and Mary. You might want to give your child a rosary if he or she does not already have one.

Learn by heart **Faith Summary**

- The rosary is a special prayer Catholics pray to Mary.

- While we pray the rosary, we meditate on the joyful, sorrowful, and glorious mysteries.

Living for God's Kingdom

Jesus preached the good news of the kingdom of God. The good news is that God loves us and is always with us in our lives. Jesus showed us that we live for God's kingdom when we do God's loving will.

We take responsibility for loving and caring for others. We make a decision to live a life of love, peace, and justice for all, as Jesus showed us.

The Virtues of Faith, Hope, and Love

Faith, hope, and love are great Christian virtues. A virtue is a habit of doing good.

We have faith in God. We believe and trust in God.

We have hope in God, too. We know that he will always help us, no matter what happens. We have hope because God wants us to enjoy eternal life, which lasts forever.

Love enables us to love God, ourselves, and our neighbors as ourselves.

Practicing the virtues of faith, hope, and love helps us to work together for God's kingdom.

The Church, Jesus' Community

Jesus promised his disciples that he would send them a Helper. After Jesus returned to his Father, the Holy Spirit came on Pentecost to the disciples as their Helper.

The Holy Spirit guides us and helps our Church to live as Jesus showed us. Our Church preaches, serves, worships, and cares for all people. We belong to Jesus' community by belonging to the Catholic Church.

The Beatitudes

The Beatitudes are ways of living that Jesus gave us to be truly happy. The Holy Spirit helps us to have the courage to choose to live the Beatitudes.

Review the chart on page 50.

Living as Our Best Selves

Jesus told us that we will be judged by the way we treat one another. The Corporal and Spiritual Works of Mercy guide us in treating others as Jesus taught us. Review the charts on pages 56 and 58.

When we live the Corporal and Spiritual Works of Mercy, we bring justice and mercy to all people. We live as our best selves. We help to bring about God's kingdom.

29 UNIT 1 · TEST

Circle the letter beside the answer.

1. Jesus preached about the
   a. rosary.
   b. holy days of obligation.
   c. good news of God's kingdom.

2. Faith, hope, and love are
   a. laws of the Church.
   b. virtues.
   c. beatitudes.

3. The Holy Spirit
   a. came on Good Friday.
   b. guides and helps the Church.
   c. is the first Person of the Blessed Trinity.

4. The Beatitudes teach us to
   a. avoid sinners.
   b. be truly happy.
   c. make a lot of money.

Answer these questions.

5. What is the kingdom, or reign, of God?

_____

_____

6. How do the Works of Mercy help us to live as Jesus taught?

_____

_____

7. Tell some ways that the Church cares for people.

_____

_____

8. What are the Beatitudes?

_____

_____

9. Name one Beatitude.

_____

10. What does it mean for you to live with hope?

_____

_____

Child's name _____

Your child has just completed Unit 1. Mark and return the checklist to the catechist. It will help both you and the catechist know how to help your child's growth in faith.

____ My child needs help with the part of the Review I have underlined.

____ My child understands how we can build up the kingdom, or reign, of God.

____ I would like to speak with you. My phone number is _____.

(Signature) _____

Living as God's People

The Ten Commandments are God's laws for us today. They help us live the Law of Love. The first three commandments help us to love and honor God. The last seven help us to love others and ourselves.

Living as Free People

God gave us a free will. This means that he gave us the freedom to choose between right and wrong.

Sin is freely choosing to do what we know is wrong. We sin when we disobey God's law on purpose.

Mortal sins are very serious sins. We choose to turn away from God completely. Venial sins are less serious sins. We choose not to follow God's way but do not turn away from him completely. We can also sin by what we fail to do, or do not do.

God Is First in Our Lives

The first commandment is "I the LORD am your God, who brought you out of . . . that place of slavery. You shall not have other gods besides me" (Exodus 20:2).

We live the first commandment when we put all our faith in God and keep God first in our lives.

God's Name Is Holy

The second commandment is "You shall not take the name of the LORD, your God, in vain" (Exodus 20:7).

We do not curse. Cursing is wishing evil on someone. Swearing is calling on God to be our witness that we are telling the truth. It is a serious sin to swear on God's name and then to lie.

We live the second commandment when we respect and honor God and Jesus in all we say and do.

We Worship God

The third commandment is "Remember to keep holy the sabbath day" (Exodus 20:8). The people of Israel celebrated the Sabbath every week.

The Christian Sabbath is Sunday. Catholics have a serious obligation to attend Mass every Sunday or Saturday evening. Catholics also keep the third commandment by attending Mass on holy days of obligation.

30 UNIT 2 · TEST

Complete the sentences.

1. "You shall not take the name of the LORD, your God, in vain" is the

_____ commandment.

2. "Remember to keep holy the sabbath day" is the _____ commandment.

3. "I the Lord am your God. . . . You shall not have other gods

besides me" is the _____ commandment.

4. A very serious sin by which we turn away from God completely is

called a _____ sin.

Match.

5. All Saints   _____ January 1

6. Mary, Mother of God   _____ August 15

7. Assumption of Mary   _____ December 25

8. Immaculate Conception   _____ March 17

9. Christmas   _____ December 8

                                      _____ November 1

Think and respond.

10. How will you try to keep God first in your life?

_____

31 FIRST SEMESTER · REVIEW

Chapter 1—Living for God's Kingdom

- Jesus preached the good news of the kingdom of God.
- The kingdom of God is the saving power of his life and love in the world.
- We build up the kingdom of God by working for love, justice, and peace in our world.

Chapter 2—The Virtues of Faith, Hope, and Love

- Faith enables us to believe and trust in God.
- Hope enables us to have full confidence in God, no matter what happens.
- Love enables us to love God, ourselves, and our neighbors.

Chapter 3—The Church, Jesus' Community

- The Church is guided by the Holy Spirit.
- The Church preaches, serves, worships, and lives as Jesus' community of faith, hope, and love.
- We become members of the Church through Baptism.

Chapter 4—The Beatitudes

- The Beatitudes teach us how to follow Jesus and be truly happy.
- The Holy Spirit helps us to live the Beatitudes.
- The Beatitudes are the spirit of love, mercy, and generosity required of Jesus' disciples.

Chapter 5—Living as Our Best Selves

- The Corporal Works of Mercy are ways we care for one another's physical needs.
- The Spiritual Works of Mercy are ways we care for one another's spiritual needs.
- As disciples of Jesus, we must live the Corporal and Spiritual Works of Mercy.

Chapter 8—Living as God's People

- God gave Moses the Ten Commandments to give to the people.
- The Ten Commandments help us to live with true freedom as God's people.
- The Ten Commandments help us to live the Law of Love, which Jesus taught.

Chapter 9—Living as Free People

- We can sin in thought, word, or action.
- Very serious sins are called mortal sins; less serious sins are called venial sins.
- A sin is mortal when what we do is very seriously wrong; we know that it is very wrong and that God forbids it; we freely choose to do it.

Chapter 10—God Is First in Our Lives

- The first commandment is "I, the LORD, am your God, who brought you out of . . . that place of slavery. You shall not have other gods besides me."
- Jesus taught us to put God first in our lives.
- When we live the first commandment, we live in true freedom.

Chapter 11—God's Name Is Holy

- The second commandment is "You shall not take the name of the LORD, your God, in vain."
- We live the second commandment by respecting God's name, the name of Jesus, and holy places.
- Cursing is wishing evil on someone. Swearing is calling on God to be our witness that we are telling the truth.

Chapter 12—We Worship God

- The third commandment is "Remember to keep holy the sabbath day."
- Christians celebrate their Sabbath on Sunday. We remember that Jesus rose from the dead on Easter Sunday.
- Catholics must take part in the Mass on Sunday or Saturday evening and on all holy days of obligation.

31 FIRST SEMESTER · TEST

Circle the letter beside the answer.

1. The eight guidelines that teach us to be happy are the
   a. Ten Commandments.
   b. Beatitudes.
   c. Works of Mercy.
   d. Gospels.

2. The Holy Spirit came upon the disciples on
   a. Easter.
   b. Ascension Thursday.
   c. Pentecost.
   d. Good Friday.

3. On Mount Sinai Moses received the
   a. Beatitudes.
   b. Works of Mercy.
   c. Ten Commandments.
   d. Bible.

4. When we disobey God's law on purpose we
   a. sin.
   b. make a mistake.
   c. are tempted.
   d. have an accident.

5. The ——— is God's word.
   a. virtues
   b. scrolls
   c. Laws of the Church
   d. Bible

6. Ways of caring for the needs of others are called the Works of
   a. Faith.
   b. Hope.
   c. Mercy.
   d. Happiness.

7. Faith, hope, and love are
   a. virtues.
   b. Beatitudes.
   c. Corporal Works of Mercy.
   d. Spiritual Works of Mercy.

8. We become members of the Church at
   a. Reconciliation.
   b. Holy Communion.
   c. birth.
   d. Baptism.

9. God's rule in our lives is
   a. the kingdom of God.
   b. reconciliation.
   c. sin.
   d. temptation.

10. The first three commandments help us to love and serve
    a. others.
    b. ourselves.
    c. God.
    d. the Church.

Define each of the following terms.

11. Faith

_____

_____

_____

12. False gods

_____

_____

_____

13. Pentecost

_____

_____

_____

14. Free will

_____

_____

_____

15. Respect

_____

_____

16. Sin

_____

_____

_____

17. Ten Commandments

_____

_____

_____

18. Scriptures

_____

_____

_____

19. Beatitudes

_____

_____

_____

20. God's will

_____

_____

Loving Our Parents

In the fourth commandment God tells us, "Honor your father and your mother." The fourth commandment teaches us to honor and obey all those who care for us and to respect older people. We are to be good citizens and obey the just laws of our country.

Living for Life

God wants us to respect all living things. The fifth commandment is "You shall not kill." This commandment teaches us that human life is sacred. Human beings are made in the image and likeness of God. We respect and care for our bodies.

We live the fifth commandment when we care about life all over the world.

Faithful in Love

The sixth and ninth commandments help married couples to be faithful to each other. The sixth commandment is "You shall not commit adultery." *Adultery* means being unfaithful to one's wife or husband. The ninth commandment is "You shall not covet your neighbor's wife or husband." *Covet* means want.

The sixth and ninth commandments teach us to respect our bodies and the bodies of other people. Loving others faithfully now prepares us to love someone forever in marriage.

Sharing Our Things

God wants us to share our good things with others. Because people can be selfish and greedy, God gives us the seventh commandment, "You shall not steal." It is wrong to take what does not belong to us. We must respect and treat with care things that belong to others.

The tenth commandment is "You shall not covet your neighbor's house . . . nor anything else that belongs to him." We must not be so jealous of another's things that we would steal or damage them if we could. If we want to follow Jesus, we work to see that all people have their fair share of what they need to live.

Living and Telling the Truth

God wants us to be truthful. The eighth commandment is "You shall not tell lies against your neighbor." This commandment teaches us that it is wrong to lie, to tell someone's secrets, and to gossip.

UNIT 3 ▪ TEST

Circle the letter beside the answer.

1. The fourth commandment teaches us
   a. to work for justice.
   b. to respect life.
   c. to obey our parents.
   d. to be fair.

2. When we love another faithfully, we
   a. are loyal and true.
   b. obey the seventh commandment.
   c. obey the fourth commandment.
   d. live the Beatitudes.

3. When we steal we do something that is
   a. wrong only if we get caught.
   b. against the seventh commandment.
   c. against the fourth commandment.
   d. not wrong.

4. The eighth commandment teaches us
   a. to honor our parents.
   b. to choose life.
   c. to be truthful.
   d. to be faithful in love.

Answer these questions.

5. What is the fifth commandment?

_____

6. How can you show respect for life?

_____

_____

7. How will you be a faithful friend?

_____

_____

8. Why is telling the truth important?

_____

_____

9. How can you show you have respect for the possessions of others?

_____

_____

10. How should we honor those who care for us?

_____

_____

Child's name _____

Your child has just completed Unit 3. Mark and return the checklist to the catechist. It will help both you and the catechist know how to help your child's growth in faith.

My child needs help with the part of the Review I have underlined.

My child understands how the commandments help us to live as God's people.

I would like to speak with you. My phone number is _____.

(Signature) _____

The Spirit Gives Us Life

To help us, the Holy Spirit gives us the gifts of wisdom, understanding, right judgment, courage, knowledge, reverence, and wonder and awe. The Holy Spirit guides and helps everyone in the Church to live for the kingdom, or reign, of God.

The Church Guides Us

Jesus called his disciples to be his Church. Everyone in the Church must work for the kingdom of God.

Some people are called to be leaders in our Church. The pope, the successor of Saint Peter, is the leader of the whole Catholic Church. The bishop is the leader of the diocese. The pastor is the priest who is the leader of a parish.

Many other people also serve as leaders in our Church.

Examining Our Conscience

Our conscience is the ability we have to decide whether something is right or wrong.

An examination of conscience is asking ourselves, with the help of the Holy Spirit, how well we have obeyed God's law and have loved and served others.

We Celebrate Reconciliation

Jesus gave his disciples the power to forgive sins in God's name. In the sacrament of Reconciliation, our bishops and priests act in the name of God and the Christian community to forgive our sins.

These are two ways we can take part in the sacrament of Reconciliation: by ourselves with the priest (Individual Rite) or with others in our parish and the priest (Communal Rite).

We Celebrate the Eucharist

We gather together and begin the Mass by asking God's forgiveness. In the Liturgy of the Word, we listen carefully as God speaks to us through the different readings from the Bible. After the Creed, we pray for the whole Church in the prayer of the faithful.

The Liturgy of the Eucharist is our great prayer of praise and thanks. Through the power of the Holy Spirit and the words and actions of the priest, the bread and wine become the Body and Blood of Christ. We receive Jesus in Holy Communion.

33 UNIT 4 · TEST

Complete these sentences.

1. The seven powerful signs through which Jesus shares God's life and love with us are called the

_____.

2. The Helper who guides each Christian and the whole Church is the

_____.

3. The ability we have to decide whether something is right or wrong is called

_____.

4. The pardon we receive in Reconciliation is called

_____.

5. The leader of the whole Church is the

_____.

6. We celebrate God's forgiveness and mercy in the sacrament of

_____.

7. The bishop is the leader of our

_____.

Think and respond.

8. How does the Holy Spirit help Christians live as followers of Jesus?

_____

_____

_____

9. Write what happens during the Liturgy of the Word at Mass.

_____

_____

_____

10. How can you live for the kingdom of God?

_____

_____

_____

34 SECOND SEMESTER ▪ REVIEW

Chapter 15—Loving Our Parents

- The fourth commandment is "Honor your father and your mother."

- Jesus showed us how to keep the fourth commandment.

- The fourth commandment teaches us to honor and obey all who take care of us.

Chapter 16—Living for Life

- The fifth commandment is "You shall not kill." It teaches us that all human life is sacred.

- All people have an equal right to life and to be treated with justice.

- We choose life when we care for all people and the world around us.

Chapter 17—Faithful in Love

- The sixth commandment is "You shall not commit adultery." The ninth commandment is "You shall not covet your neighbor's wife."

- We do not do anything to our own body or to another person's body that is disrespectful in thought, word, or action.

- To be faithful means to be loyal and true to someone.

Chapter 18—Sharing Our Things

- The seventh commandment is "You shall not steal." The tenth commandment is "You shall not want to take your neighbor's possessions."

- We are responsible for God's gift of creation.

- We must share with people less fortunate than ourselves.

Chapter 19—Living and Telling the Truth

- The eighth commandment is "You shall not bear false witness against your neighbor."

- This commandment teaches us that it is wrong to lie, to tell someone's secrets, or to gossip.

- A person who has the courage to tell and live the truth is a true disciple of Jesus Christ.

Chapter 22 — The Spirit Gives Us Life

- God the Holy Spirit fills each of us with special gifts.

- The gifts of the Holy Spirit are wisdom, understanding, right judgment, courage, knowledge, reverence, and wonder and awe.

- When we pray for guidance, God the Holy Spirit will help us to make the right choices.

Chapter 23 — The Church Guides Us

- The Holy Spirit guides the whole Church in continuing Jesus' mission.

- Each baptized person has something special to do to carry on Jesus' mission.

- The laws of the Church help us to live as good Catholics.

Chapter 24 — Examining Our Conscience

- Our conscience helps us to decide what is right and wrong.

- With the help of the Holy Spirit, we examine our conscience by asking ourselves how well we have lived God's law.

- We examine our conscience before celebrating the sacrament of Reconciliation.

Chapter 25 — We Celebrate Reconciliation

- We celebrate God's mercy and forgiveness in the sacrament of Reconciliation.

- We can take part in the sacrament of Reconciliation alone with the priest or with the community and the priest.

- Jesus asks us to be reconcilers in our family, neighborhood, and world.

Chapter 26 — We Celebrate the Eucharist

- The Mass is made up of the Liturgy of the Word and the Liturgy of the Eucharist.

- We listen to readings from the Bible during the Liturgy of the Word.

- During the Liturgy of the Eucharist the bread and wine become the Body and Blood of Christ.

Circle the letter beside the answer.

1. "You shall not kill" is the
   a. first commandment.
   b. fourth commandment.
   c. fifth commandment.
   d. sixth commandment.

2. "Not have other gods besides me" is the
   a. first commandment.
   b. second commandment.
   c. sixth commandment.
   d. ninth commandment.

3. "You shall not steal" is the
   a. sixth commandment.
   b. seventh commandment.
   c. eighth commandment.
   d. tenth commandment.

4. "Remember to keep holy the sabbath day" is the
   a. second commandment.
   b. third commandment.
   c. fifth commandment.
   d. sixth commandment.

5. "You shall not covet your neighbor's wife" is the
   a. second commandment.
   b. third commandment.
   c. fifth commandment.
   d. ninth commandment.

6. "You shall not commit adultery" is the
   a. first commandment.
   b. fourth commandment.
   c. sixth commandment.
   d. ninth commandment.

7. "Honor your father and mother" is the
   a. fourth commandment.
   b. eighth commandment.
   c. ninth commandment.
   d. tenth commandment.

8. "You shall not take the name of the LORD, your God, in vain" is the
   a. first commandment.
   b. second commandment.
   c. eighth commandment.
   d. tenth commandment.

9. "You shall not covet your neighbor's house . . ." is the
   a. fifth commandment.
   b. seventh commandment.
   c. ninth commandment.
   d. tenth commandment.

10. "You shall not bear false witness against your neighbor" is the
    a. fifth commandment.
    b. seventh commandment
    c. eighth commandment.
    d. tenth commandment.

Define each of the following terms.

11. Conscience

_____

_____

12. Sin

_____

_____

13. Sacred

_____

_____

14. Absolution

_____

_____

15. Laws of the Church

_____

_____

16. Marriage vow

_____

_____

Answer.

17. Name two gifts of the Holy Spirit.

_____

_____

18. Write one law of the Church.

_____

_____

19. Name the two main parts of the Mass.

_____

_____

20. What does it mean for you to do God's loving will?

_____

_____

_____

◀ OPENING ACTIVITY ▶

Choose teams to do this activity. Each team will be given a slip of paper on which is written a rule or a law. For example: "Keep off the grass." Team members will decide how to pantomime the rule, and then act it out for the whole group. Allow thirty seconds of "guessing time." Use a timer if you have one.

When all the pantomimes have been completed, look back over the rules or laws presented. Ask yourselves these questions:

- Is this rule (law) a good one or a bad one? Why?
- What kinds of rules or laws help us to live in true freedom?
- What kinds of rules or laws take away true freedom?

Share your thoughts as a group.

◀ **THINKING ABOUT GOD'S LAWS** ▶

Now talk about these questions with your team:

● How does keeping the commandments help you to love God? yourself? others?

Choose a team member to record on newsprint your team's responses. After five minutes, all the teams should come together to share responses. One person from each team should give a summary of what his or her team members said.

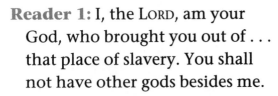

Leader: As disciples of Jesus Christ, we are all called to live the Ten Commandments. Living these laws will help us to become people of justice and peace and to love God, ourselves, and our neighbors as ourselves.

Reader 1: I, the LORD, am your God, who brought you out of . . . that place of slavery. You shall not have other gods besides me.

Reader 2: You shall not take the name of the LORD, your God, in vain.

Reader 3: Remember to keep holy the Sabbath day.

Reader 4: Honor your father and your mother.

Reader 5: You shall not kill.

Reader 6: You shall not commit adultery.

Reader 7: You shall not steal.

Reader 8: You shall not bear false witness against your neighbor.

Reader 9: You shall not covet your neighbor's wife.

Reader 10: You shall not covet your neighbor's house . . . .

All: God, be with us today as we think about the Ten Commandments and how they can help us to live as your disciples. We ask this in the name of Jesus Christ, who lives and reigns forever and ever. Amen.

◀ JOURNALING ▶

Take time now to think about God's laws in your own life. Let yourself become very quiet and still. Breathe deeply. Then think about the commandment that you find the most difficult to obey. Why do you think this is so? Would you like to do better with it? Do you think God will help you do better? What will you ask of God in prayer?

Write your thoughts as a prayer in your journal as quiet music plays in the background.

Divide into teams of five or six and choose one of the following projects:

● **Word Collage**

From poster board cut out a large circle. Decorate it to represent the earth. Then, on sheets of colored construction paper, write words that describe the feelings that come from following the Ten Commandments. Cut these words out and paste them to the "earth."

● **Footsteps to Follow Jesus**

On drawing paper sketch a path of ten footsteps. On each footstep write one of the commandments and how you or your group can live it.

● **Justice and Peace Collage**

On a large piece of poster board draw large block letters that spell out the word PEACE. Use magazines and newspapers to look for pictures that show people living the commandments. Cut out pictures that represent people doing acts of justice to bring about peace. Paste them within the word PEACE. Take time to have one person from each team explain the collages to the entire group.

◀ PRAYER SERVICE ▶

Leader: Loving God, living the Law of Love and following the Ten Commandments brings us true freedom. With this freedom we pray. . .

All: Loving God, fill us with your love and peace.

Leader: For the people in our world, that we can help one another to put God first in our lives, let us pray to the Lord.

All: Loving God, fill us with your love and peace.

Leader: For our Christian community, that we can help bring about God's kingdom of justice and peace, let us pray to the Lord.

All: Loving God, fill us with your love and peace.

Leader: For our parish family, that together we may grow stronger, wiser, happier, and more faithful in our lives as Catholics, let us pray to the Lord.

All: Loving God, fill us with your love and peace.

Leader: For our families, that we may show respect for other people who do God's will, let us pray to the Lord.

All: Loving God, fill us with your love and peace.

Leader: Loving God, when we obey out of love, we know the peace that comes from doing your will. Help us always to follow the road that leads to your peace. Amen.

Conclude by joining together as a group to sing a song of peace (for example, "Let There Be Peace on Earth").

Sharing Our Faith as Catholics

God is close to us at all times and in all places, calling us and helping us in coming to faith. When a person is baptized and welcomed into the faith community of the Church, everyone present stands with family and other members of the parish. We hear the words, "This is our faith. This is the faith of the Church. We are proud to profess it, in Christ Jesus our Lord." And we joyfully answer, "Amen"—"Yes, God, I believe."

The Catholic Church is our home in the Christian community. We are proud to be Catholics, living as disciples of Jesus Christ in our world. Each day we are called to share our faith with everyone we meet, helping to build up the kingdom, or reign, of God.

What is the faith we want to live and to share? Where does the gift of faith come from? How do we celebrate it and worship God? How do we live it? How do we pray to God? In these pages, you will find a special faith guide written just for you. It can help you as a fourth grader to grow in your Catholic faith and to share it with your family and with others, too.

Following the Church's teachings and what God has told us in the Bible, we can outline some of our most important beliefs and practices in four ways:

WHAT WE BELIEVE — CREED

HOW WE CELEBRATE — SACRAMENTS

HOW WE LIVE — MORALITY

HOW WE PRAY — PRAYER

CATHOLICS BELIEVE...

THERE IS ONE GOD IN THREE DIVINE PERSONS: Father, Son, and Holy Spirit. One God in three divine Persons is called the Blessed Trinity; it is the central teaching of the Christian religion.

GOD THE FATHER is the creator of all things.

GOD THE SON took on human flesh and became one of us. This is called the incarnation. Our Lord Jesus Christ, who is the Son of God born of the Virgin Mary, proclaimed the kingdom of God. Jesus gave us the new commandment of love and taught us the way of the Beatitudes. We believe that by his sacrifice on the cross, he died to save us from the power of sin—original sin and our personal sins. He was buried and rose from the dead on the third day. Through his resurrection we share in the divine life, which we call grace. Jesus, the Christ, is our Messiah. He ascended into heaven and will come again to judge the living and the dead.

GOD THE HOLY SPIRIT is the third Person of the Blessed Trinity, adored together with the Father and Son. The action of the Holy Spirit in our lives enables us to respond to the call of Jesus to live as faithful disciples.

We believe in **ONE, HOLY, CATHOLIC, AND APOSTOLIC CHURCH** founded by Jesus on the "rock," which is Peter, and the other apostles.

As Catholics, **WE SHARE A COMMON FAITH.** We believe and respect what the Church teaches: everything that is contained in the word of God, both written and handed down to us.

We believe in the **COMMUNION OF SAINTS** and that we are to live forever with God.

I have also learned this year that to believe as a Catholic means

_____

_____

CATHOLICS CELEBRATE...

S A C R A M E N T S

THE CHURCH, THE BODY OF CHRIST, continues the mission of Jesus Christ throughout human history. Through the sacraments and by the power of the Holy Spirit, the Church enters into the mystery of the death and resurrection of the Savior and the life of grace.

THE SEVEN SACRAMENTS are Baptism, Confirmation, Eucharist, Holy Orders, Matrimony, Reconciliation, and Anointing of the Sick. Through the sacraments, we share in God's grace so that we may live as disciples of Jesus.

By participating in the celebration of the sacraments, Catholics grow in holiness and in living as disciples of Jesus. Freed from sin by Baptism and strengthened by Confirmation, we are nourished by Christ himself in the Eucharist. We also share in God's mercy and love in the sacrament of Reconciliation.

CATHOLICS CELEBRATE THE EUCHARIST AT MASS. They do this together with a priest. The priest has received the sacrament of Holy Orders and acts in the person of Christ, our High Priest. The Mass is a meal and a sacrifice. It is a meal because in the Mass Jesus, the Bread of Life, gives us himself to be our food. Jesus is really present in the Eucharist. The Mass is a sacrifice, too, because we celebrate Jesus' death and resurrection and remember all that he did for us to save us from sin and to bring us new life. In this great sacrifice of praise, we offer ourselves with Jesus to God.

THE EUCHARIST IS THE SACRAMENT OF JESUS' BODY AND BLOOD. It is the high point of Catholic worship. It is a great privilege to take part weekly in the celebration of the Mass with our parish community.

I have also learned this year that to celebrate as a Catholic means

_____

_____

CATHOLICS LIVE...

WE ARE MADE IN THE IMAGE AND LIKENESS OF GOD and are called to live as disciples of Jesus Christ. Jesus said to us, "Love one another as I have loved you."

When we live the way Jesus showed us and follow his teachings, we can be truly happy and live in real freedom.

To help us live as Jesus' disciples, we are guided by the Law of Love, the Beatitudes, and the Ten Commandments. The Works of Mercy and the Laws of the Church also show us how to grow in living as Jesus' disciples.

Together with our Jewish brothers and sisters and all Christians everywhere, Catholics try to obey and live by **THE TEN COMMANDMENTS.** These are the laws God gave to Moses to help God's people keep their covenant with him.

The first commandment tells us to keep God first in our lives.

The second commandment tells us to respect God's holy name and the holy name of Jesus.

The third commandment tells us to keep the Sabbath as a holy day. It reminds Catholics of our serious obligation to take part in Mass each week.

The fourth commandment tells us to love and honor our parents, guardians, and all who lead and care for us.

The fifth commandment tells us to respect all life, especially human life. We are to care for our bodies and treat others with kindness and respect.

The sixth and ninth commandments tell us to be faithful people. We are never to do anything to our bodies or the bodies of others that is disrespectful in thought, word, or action.

The seventh and tenth commandments tell us to be just and not to take what belongs to others. We are to share what we can with those less fortunate.

The eighth commandment tells us that we must be people who tell and live the truth and not lie or gossip.

As members of the Church, the body of Christ, we are guided by the **CHURCH'S TEACHINGS** that help us to form our conscience. These teachings have come down to us from the time of Jesus and the apostles and have been lived by God's people throughout history. We share them with millions of Catholics throughout the world.

Through **PRAYER AND THE SACRAMENTS,** especially Eucharist and Reconciliation, we are strengthened to live as Jesus asked us to live. In faith, hope, and love, we as Catholic Christians are called not just to follow rules. We are called to live a whole new way of life as disciples of Jesus.

In living as Jesus' disciples, **WE ARE CHALLENGED EACH DAY TO CHOOSE BETWEEN RIGHT AND WRONG.** Even when we are tempted to make wrong choices, the Holy Spirit is always present to help us make the right choices. Like Jesus, we are to live for God's kingdom, or reign. Doing all this means that we live a Christian moral life. As Christians we are always called to follow the way of Jesus.

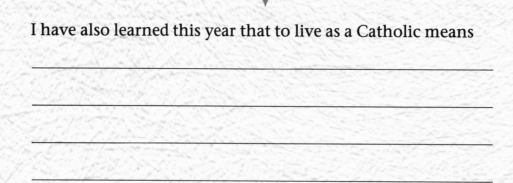

I have also learned this year that to live as a Catholic means

_____

_____

_____

_____

CATHOLICS PRAY...

PRAYER IS TALKING AND LISTENING TO GOD. We pray prayers of thanksgiving and sorrow; we praise God, and we ask God for what we need as well as for the needs of others.

WE CAN PRAY IN MANY WAYS AND AT ANY TIME. We can pray using our own words, words from the Bible, or just by being quiet in God's presence. We can also pray with song or dance or movement.

WE ALSO PRAY THE PRAYERS OF OUR CATHOLIC FAMILY that have come down to us over many centuries. Some of these prayers are the Our Father, the Hail Mary, the Glory to the Father, the Apostles' Creed, the Angelus, the Hail Holy Queen, and Acts of Faith, Hope, Love, and Contrition. Catholics also pray the rosary while meditating on events in the lives of Jesus and Mary.

As members of the Catholic community, we participate in the great liturgical prayer of the Church, **THE MASS.** We also pray with the Church during **THE LITURGICAL SEASONS OF THE CHURCH YEAR**—Advent, Christmas, Lent, the Triduum, Easter, and Ordinary Time.

In prayer, we are joined with the whole communion of saints in praising and honoring God.

I have also learned this year that to pray as a Catholic means

_____

_____

_____

_____

PRAYER

By this time, you should know many of these prayers and practices by heart.

Our Father

Our Father, who art in heaven,
hallowed be thy name;
thy kingdom come;
thy will be done on earth
as it is in heaven.
Give us this day our daily bread;
and forgive us our trespasses
as we forgive those
who trespass against us;
and lead us not into temptation,
but deliver us from evil. Amen.

Hail Mary

Hail Mary, full of grace,
the Lord is with you;
blessed are you among women,
and blessed is the fruit
of your womb, Jesus.
Holy Mary, Mother of God,
pray for us sinners now
and at the hour of our death. Amen.

Act of Contrition

My God,
I am sorry for my sins with all my heart.
In choosing to do wrong
and failing to do good,
I have sinned against you
whom I should love above all things.
I firmly intend, with your help,
to do penance,
to sin no more,
and to avoid whatever leads me to sin.
Our Savior Jesus Christ
suffered and died for us.
In his name, my God, have mercy.

Glory to the Father

Glory to the Father, and to the Son,
and to the Holy Spirit.
As it was in the beginning,
is now, and will be for ever. Amen.

Apostles' Creed

I believe in God, the Father Almighty,
creator of heaven and earth.

I believe in Jesus Christ,
his only Son, our Lord.
He was conceived by the power
of the Holy Spirit
and born of the Virgin Mary.
He suffered under Pontius Pilate,
was crucified, died, and was buried.
He descended to the dead.
On the third day he rose again.
He ascended into heaven,
and is seated at the right hand
of the Father.
He will come again to judge
the living and the dead.

I believe in the Holy Spirit,
the holy catholic Church,
the communion of saints,
the forgiveness of sins,
the resurrection of the body,
and the life everlasting. Amen.

Morning Offering

O Jesus, I offer you all my prayers,
works, and sufferings of this day
for all the intentions of your most
Sacred Heart. Amen.

Holy, Holy, Holy

Holy, holy, holy Lord
    God of power and might,
heaven and earth are full
        of your glory
    Hosanna in the highest.
Blessed is he who comes
        in the name of the Lord.
    Hosanna in the highest.

Prayer to the Holy Spirit

Come, Holy Spirit,
fill the hearts of your faithful,
and enkindle in them
the fire of your love.
Send forth your Spirit and they
shall be created, and you shall
renew the face of the earth.

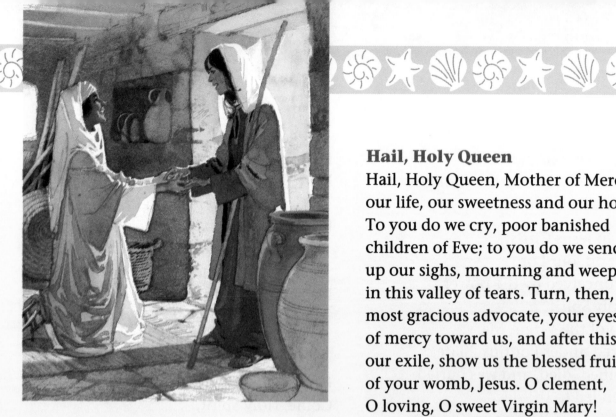

The Angelus
The angel of the Lord declared to Mary,
and she conceived by the Holy Spirit.
Hail Mary....

Behold the handmaid of the Lord,
be it done to me according to your word.
Hail Mary....

And the Word was made flesh
and dwelled among us.
Hail Mary....

Pray for us, O Holy Mother of God,
that we may be made worthy of
the promises of Christ.

Let us pray:
Pour forth, we beseech you, O Lord, your
grace into our hearts that we to whom
the incarnation of Christ your Son was
made known by the message of an angel
may, by his passion and death, be
brought to the glory of his resurrection,
through Christ our Lord.
Amen.

Hail, Holy Queen
Hail, Holy Queen, Mother of Mercy,
our life, our sweetness and our hope!
To you do we cry, poor banished
children of Eve; to you do we send
up our sighs, mourning and weeping
in this valley of tears. Turn, then,
most gracious advocate, your eyes
of mercy toward us, and after this
our exile, show us the blessed fruit
of your womb, Jesus. O clement,
O loving, O sweet Virgin Mary!

Prayer for Vocations
Dear God,
You have a great and loving plan
for our world and for me.
I wish to share in that plan fully,
faithfully, and joyfully.
Help me to understand what it is
you wish me to do with my life.

- Will I be called to the priesthood
  or religious life?

- Will I be called to live a married life?

- Will I be called to live the single life?

Help me to be attentive to the signs
that you give me about preparing
for the future.

And once I have heard and understood
your call, give me the strength and the
grace to follow it with generosity and
love. Amen.

The Rosary

The Five Joyful Mysteries (by custom, used on Mondays, Thursdays, and the Sundays of Advent)

1. The annunciation
2. The visitation
3. The birth of Jesus
4. The presentation of Jesus in the Temple
5. The finding of Jesus in the Temple

The Five Sorrowful Mysteries (by custom, used on Tuesdays, Fridays, and the Sundays of Lent)

1. The agony in the garden
2. The scourging at the pillar
3. The crowning with thorns
4. The carrying of the cross
5. The crucifixion and death of Jesus

The Five Glorious Mysteries (by custom, used on Wednesdays, Saturdays, and the remaining Sundays of the year)

1. The resurrection
2. The ascension
3. The descent of the Holy Spirit upon the apostles
4. The assumption of Mary into heaven
5. The coronation of Mary as queen of heaven

Blessing and Giving of Ashes

Ash Wednesday is the first day of Lent. Catholics begin the Lenten season of penance by receiving blessed ashes. Ashes are an ancient sign of sorrow for sin and repentance. On Ash Wednesday the Church uses the ashes of palms left over from Palm Sunday of the year before. The ashes are blessed and placed on our foreheads in the shape of a cross with these or similar words:
"Turn away from sin and be faithful to the Gospel," or "Remember, you are dust and to dust you will return."

Blessing and Giving of Palms

The Sunday that begins Holy Week is called Passion, or Palm, Sunday. On Palm Sunday we remember the day on which Jesus rode into Jerusalem on a donkey and was greeted by the people with great joy. They welcomed him as the Son of David, the Messiah. They broke off palm branches from the trees and waved them in the air. On this day, the Church blesses palms before Mass. The palms are given out to the people, who hold them during the reading of the gospel. Many Christians bring the palms home and keep them as a remembrance of the saving work of Jesus Christ.

The Stations of the Cross

There are fourteen "stations," or stops. At each one, we pause and think about what is happening at the station.

1. Jesus is condemned to die.
2. Jesus takes up his cross.
3. Jesus falls the first time.
4. Jesus meets his Mother.
5. Simon helps Jesus carry his cross.
6. Veronica wipes the face of Jesus.
7. Jesus falls the second time.
8. Jesus meets the women of Jerusalem.
9. Jesus falls the third time.
10. Jesus is stripped of his garments.
11. Jesus is nailed to the cross.
12. Jesus dies on the cross.
13. Jesus is taken down from the cross.
14. Jesus is laid in the tomb.

Blessed Sacrament

Catholics have a wonderful custom of going into the church to make a visit to Jesus in the Blessed Sacrament. The Blessed Sacrament is kept, or reserved, in the tabernacle for bringing Holy Communion to the sick and for worshiping Jesus Christ, who is truly present in the sacrament. We genuflect, or bend the right knee, toward the tabernacle before going into the pew. This is a sign of reverence for Jesus, who is present in the Blessed Sacrament. We can talk to Jesus about our needs, hurts, hopes, sorrows, and thanks.

Benediction of the Blessed Sacrament

Benediction is an ancient practice in the Church. The word *benediction* comes from the Latin word for "blessing." It is a gentle and peaceful ritual, reminding us that Jesus fills our lives with many blessings.

At Benediction a large Host, which was consecrated during Mass, is placed in a large holder called a "monstrance" so that all can see the Blessed Sacrament. The priest burns incense before the Blessed Sacrament. The incense is a sign of the adoration we offer in God's presence. The priest then lifts the monstrance and blesses the people. Each one makes the sign of the cross and bows in reverence before the Blessed Sacrament.

The Ten Commandments are found on page 80.

The Laws of the Church are found on page 215.

The Beatitudes are found on page 50.

The **Corporal and Spiritual Works of Mercy** are found on pages 56 and 58.

An **Examination of Conscience** is found on page 225.

CLOSING PRAYER SERVICE

Our Journey of Faith

Leader: Let us pause for a moment and remember that we are in the presence of God.

(Pause for a few moments of silent prayer.)

What a wonderful year this has been! We have learned what it means to live as Jesus' disciples. We also know what a challenge it will be to live God's law in the Ten Commandments for our whole lives. Before we complete our time together, let us make our needs known to Jesus. Our response will be, *Lord Jesus, let your Spirit be upon us.*

Reader 1: Lord Jesus, you have given us the way to true happiness in the Beatitudes. May they always be a part of our lives. (Response)

Reader 2: Jesus, our Savior, help us to live the virtues of faith, hope, and love each day. (Response)

Reader 3: Jesus, Son of God, help us to keep God first in our lives. (Response)

Reader 4: Jesus, our Brother, may we always use the name of God our Father, and your name with respect. (Response)

Reader 5: Jesus, our Bread of Life, as the Church community assembles each week to give thanks to God, help us to appreciate your real presence in the Eucharist. (Response)

Reader 6: Jesus, Son of Mary, help us to honor our parents, family, and all who guide us. (Response)

Reader 7: Jesus, Word made flesh, may we always respect all life. (Response)

Reader 8: Jesus, true God and true Man, help us to know that we are temples of the Holy Spirit. (Response)

Reader 9: Jesus, you are the way, the truth, and the life. Help us to share your truth with others. (Response)

Reader 10: Jesus, lover of the poor, may we care for the good things of this world and work so that others may share them in justice and peace. (Response)

Reader 11: Jesus, you are the resurrection and the life. May we always realize that keeping the Laws of the Church will help us grow as your disciples. (Response)

Leader: What is the greatest thing you have learned this year? Take a moment to thank God for it.

As friends and disciples of Jesus, let us offer one another a sign of peace.

All: Holy Trinity, one God, help us to know well what you ask of us and to put it into practice each day. In the name of the Father, and of the Son, and of the Holy Spirit. Amen.

Absolution (page 233)
Absolution is the prayer the priest says asking forgiveness of our sins.

Apostles (page 36)
The apostles were the twelve special helpers chosen by Jesus to lead the first Christian community.

Baptism (page 40)
Baptism is the sacrament by which we are freed from the power of sin, become children of God, and are welcomed into the Church, the body of Christ.

Beatitudes (page 47)
The Beatitudes are ways of living that Jesus gave us so that we can be truly happy.

Blessed Sacrament (page 294)
Another name for the Eucharist. Jesus is really present in the Blessed Sacrament.

Catholic (page 40)
The Church welcomes all people and has a message for all people.

Confirmation (page 203)
Confirmation is the sacrament in which the Holy Spirit comes to us in a special way to give us courage to live as Jesus' disciples.

Conscience (page 222)
Conscience is the ability we have to decide whether a thought, word, or deed is right or wrong. We form our conscience according to the teachings of the Church.

Consecration (page 244)
The consecration is that part of the Mass in which the bread and wine become Jesus' own Body and Blood through the power of the Holy Spirit and the words and actions of the priest.

Corporal Works of Mercy (page 56)
The Corporal Works of Mercy are ways we care for one another's physical needs.

Covenant (page 99)
In the Bible, a covenant is a special agreement made between God and people.

Disciple (page 212)
A disciple is one who learns from and follows Jesus Christ.

Eucharist (page 72)
The Eucharist is the sacrament of Jesus' Body and Blood. Jesus is really present in the Eucharist. Our gifts of bread and wine become the Body and Blood of Christ at Mass.

Examination of Conscience (page 225)
An examination of conscience is asking ourselves, with the help of the Holy Spirit, how well we have obeyed God's law and have loved and served others.

Faith (page 26)
Faith is a virtue that enables us to believe and trust in God.

Faithful (page 161)
To be faithful means to be loyal and true to someone.

Free will (page 88)
Free will means that God gives us the freedom to choose between right and wrong.

Gifts of the Holy Spirit (page 204)
The seven gifts of the Holy Spirit are wisdom, understanding, right judgment, courage, knowledge, reverence, wonder and awe. They help us to live and witness to our Catholic faith.

God's will (page 203)
God's will is what God wants us to do. We can call it God's "loving will" because he always wants what is best for us.

Grace (page 285)
Grace is a sharing in the divine life, in God's very life and love.

Greed (page 173)
Greed is wanting more than one's fair share or not wishing to share one's good fortune with others.

Heaven (page 57)
Heaven is being with God and the friends of God forever.

Hope (page 27)
Hope is a virtue that enables us to have full confidence in God, no matter what happens.

Incarnation (page 285)
The incarnation is the mystery of God "becoming flesh," or becoming one of us in Jesus Christ.

Justice (page 172)
Justice means treating all people fairly.

Kingdom of God (Reign of God) (page 19)
The kingdom, or reign, of God is the saving power of God's life and love in the world.

Law of Love (page 28)
Love the Lord your God with all your heart, with all your soul, and with all your strength. Love your neighbor as you love yourself.

Laws of the Church (page 215)
The Laws of the Church are rules by which the Church helps us to live as good Catholics and disciples of Jesus.

Liturgy (page 243)
Liturgy is the official public worship of the Church.

Liturgy of the Eucharist (page 244)
The Liturgy of the Eucharist is one of the two major parts of the Mass. It is made up of the Presentation and Preparation of the Gifts, the Eucharistic Prayer, and Holy Communion.

Liturgy of the Word (page 242)
The Liturgy of the Word is one of the two major parts of the Mass. It is made up of readings from the Old and New Testaments, Responsorial Psalm, Gospel, Homily, Creed, and Prayer of the Faithful.

Love (page 28)
Love is the virtue that enables us to love God, ourselves, and our neighbors.

Mass (page 72)
Our celebration of the Eucharist, Jesus' special meal and sacrifice.

Original sin (page 232)
Original sin is the first sin of humankind. Every human being is born with and suffers from the effects of this sin.

Penance (page 233)
We receive a penance from the priest in the sacrament of Reconciliation. Our penance helps to make up for the hurt caused by our sins and helps us to avoid sin in the future. Our penance can be a prayer or good deed.

Pope (page 213)
The pope is the bishop of Rome. He is the successor of Saint Peter and the leader of the whole Catholic Church.

Prayer (page 289)
Prayer is directing one's heart and mind to God. In prayer we talk and listen to God.

Reconciliation (page 232)
Reconciliation is the sacrament in which we celebrate God's love and forgiveness of our sins.

Respect (page 109)
To respect means to show honor to someone or something.

Sabbath (page 119)
The word *Sabbath* comes from a Jewish word that means "rest." From the beginning of the Church, Christians have celebrated their Sabbath on Sunday.

Sacrament (page 216)
The sacraments are powerful signs through which Jesus Christ shares God's life and love with us in the community of the Church.

Sacred (page 153)
Sacred means belonging to God. Human life is sacred because it belongs to God.

Sin (page 91)
Sin is freely choosing to do what we know is wrong. When we sin, we disobey God's law on purpose.

Spiritual Works of Mercy (page 58)
The Spiritual Works of Mercy are ways we care for one another's spiritual needs.

Temptation (page 90)
A temptation is a strong feeling to do or to want something wrong. Temptations are not sins.

Ten Commandments (page 79)
The Ten Commandments are laws given to us by God to help us live as God's people. God gave the Ten Commandments to Moses on Mount Sinai.

Virtue (page 27)
A virtue is the habit of doing good.

Vocation (page 212)
A vocation is our call to live holy lives of service in our Church and in our world.

Witness (page 37)
A Christian witness is one who by faith and example shares faith in Jesus Christ with others.

Worship (page 38)
Worship is praise and thanks to God in word, action, and signs.

Yahweh (page 108)
God's name as it was given to Moses. It means "I am who I am."

INDEX

* **Bold-faced** pages indicate chapters

* **Bold-faced** pages indicate chapters

† *Italics* refer to definitions

Acknowledgments

Grateful acknowledgment is due the following for their work on the Coming to Faith Program:

Maureen Gallo, Editor
Tresse De Lorenzo, Manager: Production/Art
Joe Svadlenka, Art Director
Stuart Vance, Manager: Electronic Art/Production
Dolores Keller and Walter Norfleet, Project Managers
Jeanne Whitney and Menny Borovski, Designers
Jim Saylor, Photo Editor
Mary Kate Coudal, Photo Research

Cover Photos
Myrleen Cate

Photo Credits
Diane J. Ali: 32 center right, 93.
Art Resource: 72, 257, 258.
Dennis Barnes: 210 bottom left; 237.
Black Star/ David Rubinger: 98/99; Mitch Kezar: 213 right.
Jose Carillo: 149 bottom.
Myrleen Cate: 10 right, 11, 29, 31, 32 center left, 38, 38/39, 39, 41, 58, 59, 62, 66, 67, 84, 88, 89, 90, 91, 102, 103 top, 104, 109, 142, 143, 146, 149 left, 150 center, 150 right, 151, 153, 160 bottom, 163, 164 top, 166, 172 top, 174, 176, 191, 195, 208, 210 top, 217, 226, 228, 232, 236, 238, 242, 244, 245, 248, 251 top, 256, 278, 279, 282, 283, 291.
Catholic News Service: 155, 185 top, 251 bottom right.
CROSIERS/ Gene Plaisted, OSC: 21, 36/37, 51, 83, 103 bottom, 123 top, 145, 190, 234/235, 243.
Leo de Wys: 40 background.
FPG/ Michael Kornafel: 149 top; Arthur Tilley: 150 left, 164 bottom.
Image Bank: 213 left.

Impact Visuals/ Jack Kurtz: 56 top; Jim West: 231 center.
Ken Karp: 60 left, 222, 241.
LIAISON/ Jean Claude Francolon: 19 right; Susan Greenwood: 56 bottom; Jean Michel Turpin: 210 right; Bill Pugliano: 231 top; Art Zamur: 231 bottom left; Eric Brissaud: 246.
Martha Owen, OSU: 185 bottom.
Photo Edit/ James Shaffer: 14 right; Bill Aron: 118.
Francisco J. Rangel: 260.
Steven Richter: 57 center.
Frances Roberts: 18/19, 172 bottom.
H. Armstrong Roberts: 10/11 background, 14 left, 32 top, 32 bottom, 198.
Michael Schimpf: 227.
James Shaffer: 206, 247 right.
Nancy Sheehan: 10 left, 120, 251 center right.
National Museum of Auschwitz-Birkenau Oswiecim, Poland. Courtesy of the U.S. Holocaust Memorial Museum: 250 top.
Special Olympics: 18.
Stock Market/ Mug Shots: 57 bottom; Jose Pelaez: 160 top; Tom & Dee McCarthy: 161 top.
Tony Stone Images/ Lori Adamski Peek: 28, 251 bottom left; Peter D'Angelo: 60 right; Mark Lewis: 92; Brian Bailey: 96; Steve Leonard: 108; Nicholas Parfitt: 113, 207; Penny Gentieu: 149 center; Ken Fisher: 149 right; Andy Cox: 152; John Fortunato: 161 bottom; Peter Pearson: 162; Chip Henderson: 211 bottom; Stephen Studd: 250 bottom.
SYGMA: 212.
UN Photo 185740/ J. Bu: 231 bottom right.
Viesti Associates/ Joe Viesti: 247 left.
Jim Whitmer: 57 top, 123 bottom, 211 top.

Illustrators
Blaine Martin: Cover, Digital Imaging
Wendy Pierson: Cover, Logo Rendering
Meg Aubrey: 108–109
David Barnett: 8, 26–27, 46–47, 116, 128–129, 290, 292
Andrea Barrett: 74
Teresa Berasi: 118–119, 190–191
Alex Bloch: 29, 45, 252–253
Menny Borovski: 87, 92, 211, 226, 246
Jean Bowler: 204–205
Elizabeth Brady: 80–81
Amy Bryant: 38–39, 172–173, 174, 176
Kevin Butler: 83, 107, 149, 192, 208, 210
Young Sook Cho: 212–213
Cameron Clement: 104
Gwen Connelly: 184
Neverne Covington: 201
Don Dyen: 148
Barbara Epstein Eagle: 146
Kathy Ember: 224–225
Bill Farnsworth: 16, 34–35, 280
Kristen Goeters: 65, 70–71, 220–221

Grace Goldberg: 228
Adam Gordon: 84, 143, 164–165, 175, 217, 236
Susan Greenstein: 88–89
Pat DeWitt Grush: 126, 127
Marika Hahn: 188
Brad Hamann: 31, 86, 90–91
John Haysom: 240
Ed Heins: 50, 61
Monica Higgins: 42, 52
W.B. Johnston: 17, 18–19
Jeff Jones: 114
Helen Kunze: 73
Lehner & Whyte: 194, 196–197
Victoria Lisi: 20, 158
Peg Magovern: 48–49, 106
Steve Marchesi: 78–79, 110–111
Lyn Martin: 14–15, 68
Bert Mayse: 186
Daphne McCormick: 234–235
Darlene Olivia McElroy: 13, 142–143, 152–153
David Scott Meier: 122
Lucy Montgomery: 9
Francisco X. Mora: 102
Pat Morris: 189
Cindy Patrick: 238
Bob Pepper: 178, 230
Julie Peterson: 62
Wendy Pierson: 260
Deborah Pinkney: 12, 136
Fernando Rangel: 25, 54–55, 99
Alan Reingold: 24, 44, 100–101, 180–181
Dorothy Reinhardt: 248
Lainé Roundy: 130, 244–245
Margaret Sanfilippo: 30, 119, 138, 140–141, 202–203, 252–253
Sally Schaedler: 168, 200, 256
Stephen Schudlich, 169
Evan Schwarze: 254
David Seibert: 134–135
R.J. Shay: 150–151
Bob Shein: 117, 206, 222–223
Marti Shohet: 144
Susan Spellman: 154, 182–183
Tom Sperling: 64, 132–133, 170–171
Jim Starr: 66–67, 97, 214–215, 242–243
Matt Straub: 76–77, 139, 257
Maria Stroster: 216
Peggy Tagel: 159
Mary Thelan: 124
Winson Trang: 94, 156, 281
George Ulrich: 233
Jenny Vainisi: 58–59
Gregg Valley: 162–163, 166, 218
Stuart Vance, 207
Hugh Whyte: 82
Dean Wilhite: 22, 241
Elizabeth Wolf: 179
Michael Woo: 112–113, 120, 121, 231, 251
Mary O'Keefe Young: 258–259